P · E · R · F · E · C · T
FISH
CLASSICS

P·E·R·F·E·C·T
FISH
CLASSICS

DORLING KINDERSLEY

LONDON • NEW YORK • STUTTGART • MOSCOW

A DORLING KINDERSLEY BOOK

Created and Produced by
CARROLL & BROWN LIMITED
5 Lonsdale Road
London NW6 6RA

Editorial Director Jeni Wright
Editors Sally Poole
Jennifer Feller
Norma MacMillan
Stella Vayne
Art Editor Vicky Zentner
Designers Lucy De Rosa
Mary Staples
Alan Watt
Lisa Webb
Production Editor Wendy Rogers

First published in Great Britain in 1997
by Dorling Kindersley Limited
9 Henrietta Street, London WC2E 8PS

Previously published in 1993 under the title
Look & Cook Fish Classics

Copyright © 1993, 1997 Dorling Kindersley Limited
Text copyright © 1993, 1997 Anne Willan Inc.

Visit us on the World Wide Web at http://www.dk.com

A CIP catalogue record for this book is available
from the British Library

ISBN 0-75130-0386-0

Reproduced by Colourscan, Singapore
Printed and bound in Singapore by Star Standard

CONTENTS

PERFECT FISH CLASSICS

Welcome to **Perfect Fish Classics**. This volume is designed to be the simplest, most informative cookbook you'll ever own. It is the closest I can come to sharing my techniques for cooking my own favourite recipes without actually being with you in the kitchen looking over your shoulder.

EQUIPMENT

Equipment and ingredients often determine whether or not you can cook a particular dish, so **Perfect Fish Classics** illustrates everything you need at the beginning of each recipe. You'll see at a glance how long a recipe takes to cook, how many servings it makes, what the finished dish looks like, and how much preparation can be done ahead. When you start to cook, you'll find the preparation and cooking are organized into easy-to-follow steps. Each stage is colour-coded and everything is shown in photographs with brief text to go with each step. You will never be in doubt about what it is you are doing, why you are doing it, or how it should look.

INGREDIENTS

🍽 SERVES 4-6   🥣 WORK TIME 25-35 MINUTES   🍲 COOKING TIME 20-30 MINUTES

I've also included helpful hints and ideas under "Anne Says". These may list an alternative ingredient or piece of equipment, or sometimes the reason for using a certain method is explained, or there is some advice on mastering a particular technique. Similarly, if there is a crucial stage in a recipe when things can go wrong, I've included some warnings called "Take Care".

Many of the photographs are annotated to pinpoint why certain pieces of equipment work best, or how the food should look at that stage of cooking. Because presentation is so important, a picture of the finished dish and serving suggestions are at the end of each recipe.

Thanks to all this information, you can't go wrong. I'll be with you every step of the way. So please come with me into the kitchen to look, cook, and create some delicious **Perfect Fish Classics**.

Anne Willan

WHY FISH?

*Fish continues to grow in popularity for a number of reasons: nutritionally,
it meets today's health criteria; the quality of fresh fish on the market is constantly
improving; and through better handling techniques and rapid distribution from the
oceans, lakes, and rivers the available choice is increasing. Fish seems to be a culinary
challenge, but the simplicity of the recipes in this book will surprise you, showing
fish is easy to prepare and offers endless variety, with an
enticing range of flavours and textures.*

RECIPE CHOICE

These recipes represent an array of easy fish dishes,
featuring classic favourites and contemporary flavours. All
the recipes are ideal for today's busy lifestyle, offering a
delectable selection of quick, healthy, and inventive dishes
that put the pleasure back into cooking fish. You will find
that they are all appropriate to serve as main courses, while
some could also be offered as substantial first courses.
Below is a summary of the recipes you will find in this
volume, which includes recipes based on fish fillets and
pieces of fish, as well as whole fish.

FISH FILLETS AND PIECES

*Grilled Tuna Steaks with
Salsa*: tuna steaks are
marinated, then
grilled to serve with
a colourful salsa of
tomatoes, corn, red
pepper, coriander,
and onion. *Grilled
Swordfish with
Fennel and Sun-
Dried Tomatoes*:
sun-dried tomatoes
and fennel, cooked to
melting tenderness,
complement grilled swordfish
steaks. *Crisp-Sided Salmon with Fresh Coriander Pesto*:
salmon is fried on one side only for a contrast of crunchy
skin with a lightly cooked top. The salmon is served with an
emerald-green pesto sauce made with fresh coriander.
Crisp-Sided Salmon with Garlic Sabayon: salmon fillets fried
on one side are grilled with a fluffy sabayon sauce flavoured
with garlic, white wine, and sweet vermouth. *Spicy Fish
Stew*: pieces of monkfish and a selection of vegetables mix
with apple, desiccated coconut, and plenty of spices for an
exotic casserole. *Spicy Fish Stew with Potatoes*: peas and
peanuts add crunch to this hearty haddock stew, with
potatoes for extra body. *Spicy Fish Stew with Peppers*: three
colours of pepper highlight this haddock stew. *Oriental*

*Halibut in a
Paper Case*: black
beans and Chinese
flavourings garnish
white fish fillets, baked
on a bed of crisp whole
mangetout, all enclosed in
an attractive parchment paper
package. *Thai-Style Halibut in a
Paper Case*: Thai flavourings combine with this French
cooking technique for an unusual and flavourful dish. *Tuna
and Bacon Kebabs*: cubes of tuna are marinated, wrapped in
bacon, threaded on skewers with cherry tomatoes, then
grilled to serve on a background salad of fresh spinach and
sliced mango. *Monkfish and Bacon Kebabs*: cubes of
monkfish combine with bacon and wedges of red onion for
these kebabs. *New England Cod and Mussel Chowder*:
mussels in their shells and diced bacon add colour and
flavour to this rich and creamy white fish stew. *Manhattan
Cod and Mussel Chowder*: a lively fish stew made with
tomatoes, garlic, white wine, and thyme. *Perfect Fish and
Chips*: a traditional favourite of cod fillets deep-fried in a
light beer batter, served with crisp thick-cut French fries.
Tempura-Style Fish with Sweet Potatoes: Japanese-style
coating for fish, with crisply fried sweet potato slices on
the side and an oriental dipping sauce. *Fisherman's Pie*: a
delicious combination of flaked white fish, prawns, and
hard-boiled eggs in a white sauce, topped with mashed
potato, and baked in the oven until golden brown. *Individual
Fish Crumbles*: a hearty topping
of rolled oats with parsley
and Parmesan cheese
makes a crunchy
contrast to a filling
of chunks of fish
and prawns in
white sauce
baked in
individual
casserole dishes.
*Saltimbocca of
Salmon*: this delicious
variation of traditional

veal saltimbocca uses marinated salmon slices rolled around smoked salmon and basil leaves, then sautéed in butter to serve with a tomato-basil garnish. *Paupiettes of Sole*: lemon sole fillets rolled with smoked salmon and steamed. *Roast Monkfish with Garlic and Chilli Sauces*: plump fillets of monkfish are marinated in olive oil mixed with fresh oregano and thyme, then roasted and sliced to serve with garlic and spicy chilli sauces. *Grilled Monkfish Escalopes with Garlic and Chilli Sauces*: the same pungent sauces complement thinly sliced fillets of monkfish, which are quickly cooked under a hot grill. *Seafood Lasagne*: a delicious version of lasagne made with layers of sole, prawns, scallops, and noodles, baked in a creamy sauce flavoured with mushrooms, tomatoes, shallots, and white wine and topped with cheese. *Smoked Trout and Spinach Lasagne*: pieces of smoked trout flavour this version of seafood lasagne, made colourful with green spinach pasta. *Steamed Fish Plaits with Warm Vinaigrette*: three varieties of fish are cut into strips, shaped into a delicate plait, and steamed to serve with a warm vinaigrette. *Panaché of Steamed Fish with Warm Sherry Vinaigrette*: a trio of fish with different coloured skins are steamed for this "panaché", or selection. *Monkfish Américaine*: monkfish, sometimes called "the poor man's lobster", is served in the classic sauce of tomato, garlic, white wine, and Cognac. *Salt Cod Américaine*: Américaine sauce highlights chunks of salt cod served with rice pilaf. *Turbans of Sole with Wild Mushroom Mousse*: sole fillets are wrapped turban-style around a delectable wild mushroom mousse, baked in white wine, and served with a fresh coriander butter sauce. *Turbans of Plaice with Spinach Mousse*: bright green spinach mousse is the filling for plaice fillets, with a simple tomato butter sauce as accompaniment. *Two-Colour Fish Terrine with Citrus-Ginger Sauce*: a delicate pink salmon mousseline, wrapped with white bands of sole fillet, hides a pretty mosaic of smoked salmon and sole, and is perfectly complemented by a tangy citrus sauce. *Individual Fish Terrines*: ramekins lined with thinly sliced fresh salmon fillet are filled with a smooth mousseline made with whiting or sole fillets.

WHOLE FISH

Bouillabaisse: the world-famous Mediterranean stew includes an international variety of fish, accented by saffron, garlic, fennel, orange, and Pernod. *Creole Bouillabaisse*: shellfish are added to this version of bouillabaisse, which comes from Louisiana. *Sautéed Trout with Hazelnuts*: crunchy browned hazelnuts top whole trout sautéed in butter in this rapid recipe. *Sautéed Trout with Capers, Lemon, and Croûtons*: piquant capers, lemon, and golden brown croûtons add flavour to pan-fried trout. *Poached Salmon with Watercress Sauce*: fresh salmon is poached and served whole for a dramatic presentation, with a refreshing watercress sauce on the side. *Pan-Fried Mackerel Coated in Rolled Oats*: a traditional Scottish recipe using whole mackerel cut into fillets, covered in rolled oats, and fried for a crispy coating. *Almond-Coated Rainbow Trout*: succulent trout fillets are coated with flaked almonds and pan-fried. *Grilled Trout with Orange and Mustard Glaze*: small whole fish, onions, and mushrooms are brushed with a tangy glaze of orange and mustard, then grilled. *Grilled Cod Steaks with Maître d'Hôtel Butter*: butter flavoured with chopped parsley, shallots, and lemon juice complements grilled fish steaks. *Sole Bonne Femme*: this most delicious of fish dishes is made from sole fillets poached in fish stock enriched with white wine and served with a rich mushroom and cream sauce. *Fillets of Sole with Mushrooms and Tomatoes*: mushrooms and tomatoes are added to a creamy velouté sauce topping sole fillets.

EQUIPMENT

There are many different types of fish, but you will not need many items of specialized equipment for these recipes. Most important is a fish filleting knife with a thin flexible blade, used to fillet fish, and to trim and cut it into pieces or thin slices. A chef's knife is also necessary for cutting and trimming fish and cutting up fish bones for stock. Be sure to sharpen all your knives on a steel each time you use them. Metal tongs and a metal fish slice, preferably with slots for draining, will help you turn fish fillets and pieces or transfer them from the pan.

Your baking dishes will come into use as various sizes are needed for the assortment of recipes cooked in the oven, while *Poached Salmon with Watercress Sauce* requires a large roasting tin for stove-top poaching. If you happen to have a special fish poaching pan, now is the time to use it, but a long deep flameproof dish also works well. You will need a heavy casserole or large saucepan for stews and chowders, and frying

pans for sautéed and pan-fried fish dishes. For small whole fish, such as trout, you can find special oval fish frying pans, which are pretty enough to be taken to table, although a large frying pan can be substituted. Where speciality equipment is used I have suggested easy alternatives. For example, a steamer is called for in *Steamed Fish Plaits with Warm Vinaigrette*, but a large saucepan with lid and rack can also be used. A deep-fat fryer is used in *Perfect Fish and Chips*, but a shallow saucepan can be substituted.

INGREDIENTS

Fresh fish is delicious plainly cooked, but a variety of ingredients will bring out its individual flavour.

Lemon is a favourite partner, enhancing taste whether the fish is pan-fried, steamed, or baked. Other citrus fruits, such as orange and lime, also lend their acidity to fish with delicious results. A wide range of aromatic herbs complements fish, whether they form the basis of a sauce or are sprinkled on top before or after cooking. Onion, garlic, and shallot are essential to many fish dishes, while piquant flavourings, such as fresh chillies, fresh root ginger, and capers add their own distinctive tastes. Dried spices such as cayenne pepper, cumin, coriander, cloves, saffron, and crushed chillies are more unusual, but they enliven a surprising number of recipes. Coatings for fish range beyond the standard flour, beaten egg, and breadcrumbs. Rolled oats and flaked almonds also provide a tasty covering

for fillets. Batter for deep-frying includes a leavening of beer, and white wine forms the basis of half a dozen cooking liquids and sauces.

Shellfish are natural partners for fish. Prawns and scallops combine with sole in *Seafood Lasagne*, while prawns join haddock in *Fisherman's Pie*, and oysters add authenticity to *Creole Bouillabaisse*. Mussels add zest to cod in *New England Cod and Mussel Chowder*. Vegetables play a leading role, whether as stuffing, garnish, or in a sauce. Tomatoes, with their glowing colour and touch of acid fruitiness, are ideal in sauces and salsas. Fennel is excellent with swordfish, while watercress is a good accompaniment to cold poached salmon. Spinach fills *Turbans of Plaice with Spinach Mousse*, and acts as a background salad for *Tuna and Bacon Kebabs*, while mushrooms are essential to the classic *Sole Bonne Femme*.

TECHNIQUES

A number of different techniques for preparing fish are illustrated in these recipes. Most importantly, you will learn how to prepare whole fish – how to scale them, clean them through the gills, fillet, skin, and trim them. The way to cut thin slices is illustrated, as well as how to cut up fish for soups and stews, and to purée it for a mousseline. You will also see the preparation of fish stock and court bouillon.

The recipes use a wide range of cooking methods, including poaching, grilling, and pan-frying, for whole fish, as well as fillets and smaller pieces. Tricky deep- frying is carefully explained, and steaming instructions are given for fish pieces. Baking fish in a paper case is a more unusual approach illustrated here, and a seemingly complicated fish terrine is made simple with the step-by-step pictures. Knowing how to test when fish is done is vital because few foods overcook more easily. In each recipe you'll be given the correct procedure so you cannot go wrong, no matter if you are poaching, grilling, steaming, sautéing, deep-frying, or baking in the oven.

Scale fish using back of filleting knife

GRILLED TUNA STEAKS WITH SALSA

🍽 SERVES 4 🥣 WORK TIME 25–30 MINUTES* 🍲 GRILLING TIME 5–7 MINUTES

EQUIPMENT

non-metallic shallow dish

saucepans

lemon squeezer   bowls

large metal spoon

pastry brush

slotted spoon

chef's knife

small knife

tongs

chopping board

paper towels

INGREDIENTS

tuna steaks†

corn cobs

red pepper

vegetable oil

lemon

tomatoes

limes

onion   fresh thyme

fresh coriander

† other suitable fish
huss, monkfish, swordfish

The intense heat of grilling is well suited to oily fish such as tuna, searing the outside and keeping the inside moist. Here, a tart marinade made with lemon juice deliciously offsets the richness of the tuna. A crisp, fresh salsa of tomatoes, sweetcorn, red peppers, and onion is the perfect foil.

GETTING AHEAD
The salsa can be made up to 1 day ahead and refrigerated. Grill the fish just before serving.

plus 1–2 hours marinating time

metric	SHOPPING LIST	imperial
4	tuna steaks, weighing 250 g (8 oz) each	4
	salt and pepper	
4	tomatoes	4
2	corn cobs or 200 g (6½ oz) defrosted sweetcorn kernels	2
1	medium red pepper	1
1	medium onion	1
1	medium bunch of fresh coriander	1
2	limes	2
45–60 ml	vegetable oil	3–4 tbsp
	For the marinade	
2–3	sprigs of fresh thyme	2–3
30 ml	vegetable oil	2 tbsp
½	lemon	½

ORDER OF WORK

1 MARINATE THE TUNA

2 MAKE THE SALSA

3 GRILL THE TUNA

1 MARINATE THE TUNA

1 Strip the thyme leaves from the stalks, letting them fall into the shallow dish. Add the oil to the dish.

Sprinkle salt and pepper evenly over steaks

3 Rinse the tuna steaks with cold water. Transfer to paper towels and pat dry. Season with salt and pepper. Put the tuna steaks into the marinade in the dish and turn them over, coating them well with the marinade. Cover and marinate 1–2 hours in the refrigerator, turning occasionally. While the fish is marinating, make the salsa.

2 Squeeze the juice from the lemon half and add the juice to the thyme and oil in the dish.

2 MAKE THE SALSA

1 Cut the cores from the tomatoes and score an "x" on the base of each. Immerse in a pan of boiling water until the skin starts to split. Transfer at once to a bowl of cold water. When cold, peel off the skin. Cut the tomatoes crosswise in half and squeeze out the seeds. Coarsely chop each half.

Skin splits in heat of water and makes peeling easy

Small incision speeds up splitting of tomato skin

2 Husk the corn cobs: pull the husk down each cob to the base; trim off the husk and stalk, then strip away the silky threads. Bring a large saucepan of water to a boil. Add the corn cobs to the pan, and cook them until tender, 5–7 minutes.

3 To test, lift 1 of the corn cobs out of the pan with the tongs. The kernels should pop out easily with the point of the small knife.

HOW TO CHOP AN ONION

The size of dice when chopping an onion depends on the thickness of the initial slices. For a standard size, make slices that are about 5 mm (¹/₄ inch) thick. For finely chopped onions, slice as thinly as possible.

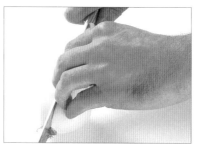

1 Peel the onion and trim the top; leave a little of the root attached.

2 Cut the onion lengthwise in half, through root and stalk.

3 Put one half, cut-side down, on the chopping board and hold the onion steady with one hand. Using a chef's knife, make a series of horizontal cuts from the top towards the root but not through it.

4 Make a series of lengthwise vertical cuts, cutting just to the root but not through it.

ANNE SAYS
"When slicing, tuck your fingertips under and use your knuckles to guide the blade of the knife."

5 Slice the onion crosswise into dice. For finely chopped onion, continue chopping until you have the fineness required.

Cut across at even intervals for neat dice

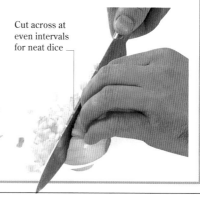

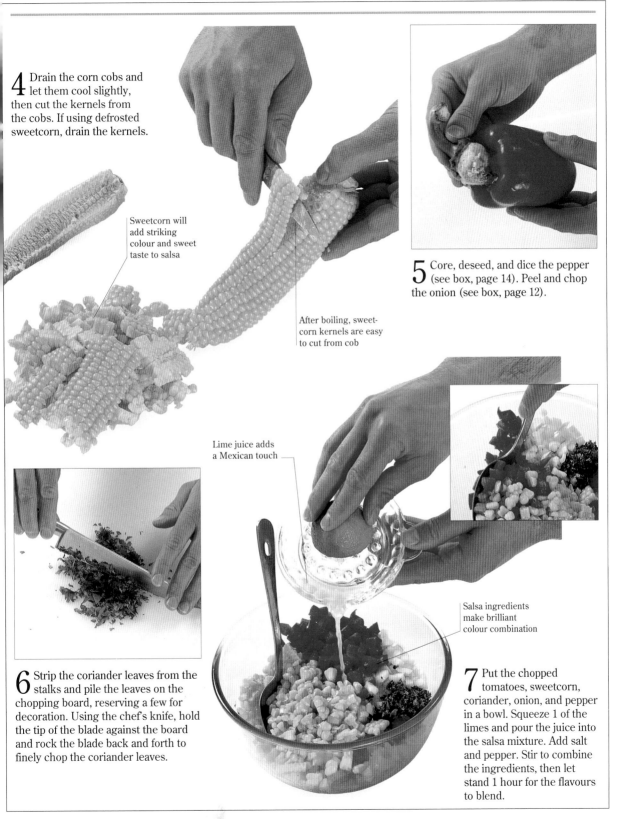

4 Drain the corn cobs and
let them cool slightly,
then cut the kernels from
the cobs. If using defrosted
sweetcorn, drain the kernels.

Sweetcorn will
add striking
colour and sweet
taste to salsa

After boiling, sweet-
corn kernels are easy
to cut from cob

5 Core, deseed, and dice the pepper
(see box, page 14). Peel and chop
the onion (see box, page 12).

Lime juice adds
a Mexican touch

Salsa ingredients
make brilliant
colour combination

6 Strip the coriander leaves from the
stalks and pile the leaves on the
chopping board, reserving a few for
decoration. Using the chef's knife, hold
the tip of the blade against the board
and rock the blade back and forth to
finely chop the coriander leaves.

7 Put the chopped
tomatoes, sweetcorn,
coriander, onion, and pepper
in a bowl. Squeeze 1 of the
limes and pour the juice into
the salsa mixture. Add salt
and pepper. Stir to combine
the ingredients, then let
stand 1 hour for the flavours
to blend.

HOW TO CORE AND DESEED A PEPPER, AND CUT IT INTO DICE

The core and seeds of peppers must always be discarded.

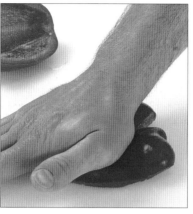

1 With a small knife, cut around the core of the pepper and pull it out. Halve the pepper lengthwise and scrape out the seeds. Cut away the white protruding ribs on the inside of the pepper.

2 Set each pepper half cut-side down on the work surface and press down firmly with the heel of your hand on top of each pepper half to flatten.

3 With a chef's knife, slice the pepper half lengthwise into strips. To dice, gather the strips together and cut across into squares.

3 GRILL THE TUNA

Pastry brush ensures even coating of marinade

Marinade on steaks gives tuna additional flavour

ANNE SAYS
"If you like, you can cook the tuna on a barbecue; it will cook just as quickly."

1 Heat the grill. Brush the grill rack with oil. Put the tuna steaks on the grill rack and brush with the marinade. Grill the steaks about 7.5 cm (3 inches) from the heat, 3–4 minutes.

2 Turn over each tuna steak, using the tongs.

3 Brush with the remaining marinade and grill 2–3 minutes longer. The tuna should be brown on the outside, but still rare in the centre. To test, flake with a knife: a translucent layer should be visible in the centre.

ANNE SAYS
"*If barbecuing, you can make an attractive criss-cross pattern on the steaks. Cook 1–2 minutes until the rack marks show, then rotate the steaks 45° and continue cooking so the marks form diamonds.*"

4 While the tuna is cooking, cut the remaining lime crosswise into thin slices with the chef's knife.

𝟙◉𝟙 TO SERVE
Arrange the tuna steaks on a bed of salsa on a platter and decorate each with a sprig of coriander. Arrange the lime slices around the tuna.

Slices of tangy lime echo salsa flavouring

Fresh coriander decorates fish

Salsa adds cool freshness to grilled tuna

GRILLED SWORDFISH WITH FENNEL AND SUN-DRIED TOMATOES

Here, swordfish steaks replace the tuna steaks. A mixture of pungent fennel and sun-dried tomatoes is the garnish, flavoured with aniseed liqueur.

1 Rinse and pat dry 4 swordfish steaks weighing 250 g (8 oz) each, then marinate as directed. Omit the salsa.

2 Wash and trim 3 fennel bulbs. Cut them lengthwise in half and slice.

3 Melt 60 g (2 oz) butter in a saucepan. Add the fennel, season with a little salt and pepper, and press a piece of buttered foil on top. Put on the lid and cook over low heat, stirring occasionally, until very soft, 40–45 minutes.

4 Drain 60 g (2 oz) sun-dried tomatoes in oil and coarsely chop them. Stir them into the fennel with 15–30 ml (1–2 tbsp) aniseed-flavoured liqueur. Continue cooking the mixture about 10 minutes, then season to taste with salt and pepper.

5 Grill the swordfish steaks as directed for the tuna steaks, and serve on warmed individual plates with the fennel mixture on the side.

CRISP-SIDED SALMON WITH FRESH CORIANDER PESTO

🍽 SERVES 4   🥣 WORK TIME 5–10 MINUTES   🍲 COOKING TIME 10–15 MINUTES

EQUIPMENT

food processor

rubber spatula

pastry brush

tweezers

chef's knife

filleting knife

palette knife

bowls

paper towels

large frying pan, preferably cast iron

cheese grater

chopping board

Good.

This is a newly popular method for cooking fish: fillets are fried until crispy on the skin side, and only lightly cooked on the top. Rich fish such as salmon and bass are particularly suitable for cooking in this way. Pesto made with fresh coriander is the perfect partner.

GETTING AHEAD
The pesto can be made up to 48 hours ahead and kept, covered, in the refrigerator. It can also be frozen. The salmon should be cooked just before serving.

metric	SHOPPING LIST	imperial
4	pieces of fresh salmon fillet, with skin, weighing about 175 g (6 oz) each	4
45 ml	vegetable oil	3 tbsp
1	lemon	1
10 ml	coarse sea salt	2 tsp
	coriander leaves	
	For the fresh coriander pesto	
1	large bunch of fresh coriander	1
2–3	garlic cloves, peeled	2–3
30 ml	pine nuts	2 tbsp
75 ml	olive oil	2½ fl oz
30 g	grated Parmesan cheese	1 oz
	salt and pepper	

INGREDIENTS

fresh salmon fillet †

Parmesan cheese   fresh coriander

pine nuts

olive oil   vegetable oil

garlic cloves

lemon   coarse sea salt

† other suitable fish
bass, mackerel, red snapper, salmon trout

ORDER OF WORK

1 MAKE THE FRESH CORIANDER PESTO

2 PREPARE AND COOK THE SALMON

MAKE THE FRESH CORIANDER PESTO

1 Put the coriander leaves in the food processor with the garlic, pine nuts, and 30 ml (2 tbsp) olive oil. Add the grated cheese.

Coriander leaves for pesto are stripped from stalks

2 With the blade of the food processor turning, slowly pour in the remaining olive oil in a thin, steady stream.

3 Continue working the ingredients in the machine until the pesto thickens and emulsifies. Season to taste with salt and pepper.

PREPARE AND COOK THE SALMON

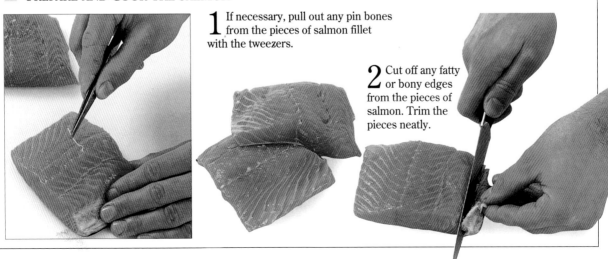

1 If necessary, pull out any pin bones from the pieces of salmon fillet with the tweezers.

2 Cut off any fatty or bony edges from the pieces of salmon. Trim the pieces neatly.

Salmon must be thoroughly dry before cooking

3 Rinse the pieces of salmon under cold running water. Transfer them to paper towels and pat dry.

Place fish skin-side down on paper towels

4 Transfer to a plate and brush the skin side of each piece of salmon fillet with some of the vegetable oil.

5 Heat the remaining oil in the frying pan until it is hot. Add the salmon fillets to the pan, placing them skin-side down.

Pink salmon contrasts in both taste and colour with green pesto

🍽 TO SERVE

Transfer the salmon fillets to warmed individual plates, sprinkle them with the sea salt, and spoon some coriander pesto beside each fillet. Decorate with twisted lemon slices and fresh coriander leaves.

6 Cook over medium heat until the skin is quite crispy and the sides are opaque, 10–15 minutes, depending on the thickness of the fillets. The top should be still slightly soft, showing that it is rare. Meanwhile, slice the lemon for decoration.

ANNE SAYS
"*If you prefer your salmon fully cooked, cover the pan, and continue cooking 1–2 minutes.*"

VARIATION

CRISP-SIDED SALMON WITH GARLIC SABAYON

The sabayon here is made in the same way as a Hollandaise sauce
with the addition of a garlic and wine flavouring.

1 To make the sauce, peel and chop 2 shallots (see box, below). Peel and chop 4 garlic cloves. Melt 15 g (½ oz) butter in a pan, add the shallots and garlic. Cook until soft, 3–5 minutes.
2 Add 15 ml (1 tbsp) double cream; bring to a boil. Add 60 ml (4 tbsp) each white wine and sweet vermouth. Cook over high heat until reduced to 30–45 ml (2–3 tbsp). Let cool slightly.
3 Melt 125 g (4 oz) butter; let cool.
4 Put 2 egg yolks and 30 ml (2 tbsp) water in a heatproof bowl; whisk until light in colour. Set over a pan of hot water; whisk until the mixture leaves a ribbon trail, 5 minutes.

5 Take the bowl from the pan of water; whisk in the butter in a slow, steady stream, leaving the milk solids from the butter at the bottom of the pan. Whisk in the garlic mixture. Season to taste with salt, white pepper, and a squeeze of lemon juice. Keep warm by setting the bowl in a pan of warm water.
6 Cook the salmon as directed; transfer to warmed individual plates. Heat the grill.
7 Spoon the garlic sabayon onto the salmon fillets to coat them. Grill about 10 cm (4 inches) from the heat until the sabayon is lightly browned, 1–2 minutes. Serve immediately.

HOW TO CHOP A SHALLOT

For a standard chop, make slices that are about 3 mm (⅛ inch) thick. For a fine chop, make the slices as thin as possible.

1 Peel the outer, papery skin from the shallot. Separate the shallot into sections if necessary.

2 Set a section flat-side down on a chopping board. Holding the shallot steady, slice horizontally, leaving the slices attached at the root.

3 Slice vertically through the shallot, again leaving the root end uncut.

Sharp chef's knife makes slicing easy

Cut just to root so shallot holds together

4 Cut across into fine dice. Continue chopping until very fine, if necessary holding the tip of the blade and rocking it up and down.

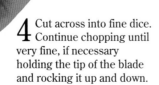

SPICY FISH STEW

 SERVES 6   WORK TIME 30–35 MINUTES   COOKING TIME 30–35 MINUTES

EQUIPMENT

 muslin†

flameproof casserole
with lid

 paper towels

saucepans, 1 with lid

 wooden spoon   small knife

slotted spoon

filleting knife

chef's knife    bowls

 vegetable peeler

apple corer   sieve

chopping board

This tasty casserole, flavoured with apple, coconut, and spices, is delicious accompanied by poppadums. Serve boiled rice on the side.

INGREDIENTS

 bay leaves

monkfish fillets†

 apple

onions

 ground
cloves   ground
cumin

vegetable
oil

garlic cloves

 desiccated
coconut

butter

tomatoes

 fish stock

celery

carrots   ground
coriander   paprika

cayenne
pepper   cornflour   ground
ginger

† other suitable fish
grey mullet, huss, red snapper

metric	SHOPPING LIST	imperial
1 kg	skinned monkfish fillets	2 lb
6	tomatoes, total weight about 1 kg (2 lb)	6
2	carrots	2
2	celery sticks	2
6	garlic cloves	6
2	medium onions	2
60 ml	vegetable oil	4 tbsp
30 ml	paprika	2 tbsp
300 ml	fish stock (see box, page 124)	½ pint
4	bay leaves	4
	salt and pepper	
	For the spicy sauce	
300 ml	fish stock	½ pint
150 g	desiccated coconut	4¾ oz
1	medium onion	1
1	apple	1
30 g	butter	1 oz
5 ml	ground cumin	1 tsp
5 ml	ground coriander	1 tsp
2.5 ml	ground ginger	½ tsp
2.5 ml	ground cloves	½ tsp
1.25 ml	cayenne pepper or 2.5 ml (½ tsp) crushed chillies	¼ tsp
22.5 ml	cornflour	1½ tbsp

ORDER OF WORK

1 MAKE THE SPICY
SAUCE

2 PREPARE THE
MONKFISH AND
VEGETABLES

3 COOK THE FISH
STEW

† tea towel can also be used

1 MAKE THE SPICY SAUCE

1 Bring the fish stock to a boil in a medium saucepan. Add the desiccated coconut.

2 Stir to mix, then cover the pan and leave the coconut to soak 30 minutes.

ANNE SAYS
"As the coconut soaks, the stock will become infused with its flavour, making coconut milk."

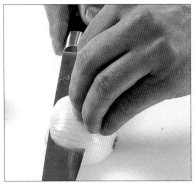

Lay each onion half flat on chopping board for dicing

Curled fingers guide knife

3 Peel the onion, leaving a little root attached, and cut lengthwise in half. Slice each half horizontally towards the root, leaving the slices attached.

4 Slice each onion half vertically, again leaving the root end uncut, then cut across to make dice.

Transfer coconut to muslin to finely strain

5 Put a large piece of muslin in the sieve, set over a bowl. Spoon in the coconut and its liquid.

6 Gather up the ends of the muslin and squeeze the coconut well to extract as much liquid or "milk" as possible. Discard the coconut and wipe the saucepan.

7 Peel the apple and core it with the apple corer. Cut the apple into halves. Cut each half horizontally into 1 cm (¹/₂ inch) slices, then cut lengthwise into strips. Cut across into dice.

Hold apple half together with fingers as you cut

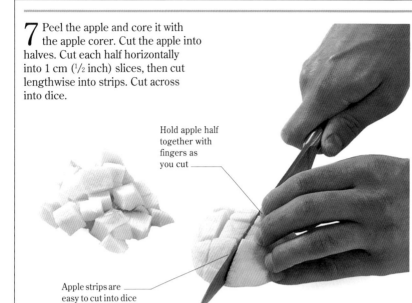

Apple strips are easy to cut into dice

8 Melt the butter in the saucepan. Add the onion and apple, and cook until soft but not brown, 3–5 minutes.

9 Add the ground cumin, coriander, ginger, cloves, and cayenne pepper to the onion and apple. Cook, stirring, over low heat, 2–3 minutes.

Paste of cornflour and coconut milk slightly thickens stew

Stir sauce constantly while adding cornflour paste

10 Put the cornflour in a small bowl. Add 30–45 ml (2–3 tbsp) of the coconut milk and blend to a smooth paste. Add remaining milk to the saucepan; bring to a boil.

11 Stir in the cornflour paste; the sauce will thicken at once. Take the pan from the heat and season the sauce to taste with salt and pepper. Set aside.

ANNE SAYS
"If the cornflour forms lumps, stir vigorously to dissolve them."

PREPARE THE MONKFISH AND VEGETABLES

1 With the filleting knife, cut away the membrane from the monkfish. Rinse the monkfish with cold water and pat dry with paper towels.

Membrane on monkfish must always be completely removed

2 Cut the fillets into 2.5 cm (1 inch) strips, then across into cubes. Set aside while preparing the vegetables.

3 Cut the cores from the tomatoes and score an "x" on the base of each with the tip of a knife. Immerse in a pan of boiling water until the skin starts to split, 8–15 seconds depending on ripeness. Using the slotted spoon, transfer at once to cold water. When cold, peel off the skin. Cut crosswise in half and squeeze out the seeds, then coarsely chop each half.

4 Peel the carrots and trim them. Cut them across into thin slices using the chef's knife.

5 Peel the strings from the celery sticks, then cut the sticks across into thin slices.

Run peeler up celery sticks to remove tough strings

6 Set the flat side of the chef's knife on top of each garlic clove and strike it with your fist. Discard the skin and finely chop the garlic. Peel the onions, leaving a little of the root attached, and cut them lengthwise in half. Cut each onion half across into thin slices.

COOK THE FISH STEW

Metal spoon is preferable to wooden spoon because it does not absorb spices

Paprika adds deep colour to fried onions

1 Heat the oil in the casserole. Add the onions and cook until soft but not brown, 3–5 minutes.

2 Add the paprika and cook, about 1 minute, stirring to combine evenly with the onions.

Carrot slices will keep shape and colour in stew

3 Add the fish stock, chopped tomatoes, garlic, bay leaves, celery, and carrots to the casserole with a little salt and pepper. Bring the mixture to a boil.

4 Reduce the heat and simmer until the liquid is reduced by one-third, 15–20 minutes.

5 Add the spicy sauce to the casserole and stir well, then bring back to a boil.

6 Add the fish. Cover and simmer, stirring occasionally, until the fish flakes easily, 12–15 minutes. Discard the bay leaves and taste for seasoning.

TO SERVE

Serve the spicy fish stew in individual warmed bowls.

Crisp poppadums perfectly complement this spicy dish

VARIATION
SPICY FISH STEW WITH POTATOES

1 Make the spicy sauce as directed in the main recipe, omitting the apple.
2 Prepare the vegetables as directed, omitting the carrots and celery.
3 Peel 2 medium potatoes and cut them into rough chunks.
4 Omit the monkfish. Prepare the same weight of haddock fillets.
5 Cook the fish stew as directed, adding the potatoes and 175 g (6 oz) fresh or defrosted green peas with the tomatoes. Continue cooking the stew as directed. Add the fish and simmer as directed, 12–15 minutes.
6 Serve in warmed individual bowls, sprinkled with coarsely chopped unsalted peanuts.

VARIATION
SPICY FISH STEW WITH PEPPERS

1 Make the spicy sauce as directed in the main recipe, omitting the apple.
2 Prepare the vegetables as directed, omitting the carrots and celery.
3 Cut out the core from 1 green, 1 red, and 1 yellow pepper, then halve the peppers and scrape out the seeds. Cut away the white ribs on the inside. Set each pepper half cut-side down on the chopping board and press with the heel of your hand to flatten it. Slice it lengthwise into medium strips.
4 Omit the monkfish. Prepare the same weight of haddock fillets.
5 Cook the fish stew as directed, adding the pepper slices with the tomatoes. Add the fish and simmer as directed, 12–15 minutes.
6 Chop a few fresh chives and sprinkle over the stew before serving.

Fish stew flavoured with rich mix of spices is a delicious and warming meal

--- **GETTING AHEAD** ---

The fish stew can be made up to 1 day ahead and kept refrigerated. Reheat it on top of the stove before serving.

ORIENTAL HALIBUT IN A PAPER CASE

🍽️ SERVES 4 🥄 WORK TIME 15–20 MINUTES 🍲 BAKING TIME 10–12 MINUTES

EQUIPMENT

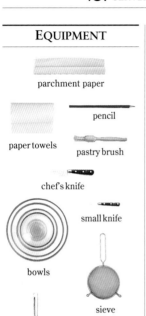

parchment paper

pencil

paper towels

pastry brush

chef's knife

small knife

bowls

sieve

kitchen scissors

colander

baking sheet

saucepan

chopping board

ANNE SAYS
"Aluminium foil can be used instead of parchment paper, but it will not puff and brown."

This recipe combines Chinese flavourings with a French cooking method. Topped with black beans and soy sauce, the fish is baked in individual paper cases. Each diner opens a paper case and savours the aroma. Cellophane noodles and stir-fried vegetables would be ideal accompaniments.

GETTING AHEAD
The filled paper cases can be prepared up to 4 hours in advance and refrigerated. Bake just before serving.

metric	SHOPPING LIST	imperial
125 g	mangetout	4 oz
2.5 cm	piece of fresh root ginger	1 inch
4	garlic cloves	4
4	spring onions	4
30 g	black fermented Chinese beans	1 oz
45 ml	light soy sauce	3 tbsp
30 ml	dry sherry	2 tbsp
2.5 ml	granulated sugar	½ tsp
15 ml	sesame oil	1 tbsp
30 ml	vegetable oil	2 tbsp
4	skinned halibut fillets or steaks, weighing about 175 g (6 oz) each	4
For the egg glaze		
1	egg	1
2.5 ml	salt	½ tsp

INGREDIENTS

halibut fillets†

black fermented Chinese beans

sesame oil

spring onions

granulated sugar

light soy sauce

egg

fresh root ginger

dry sherry

vegetable oil

mangetout

garlic cloves

† other suitable fish
cod, John Dory

ORDER OF WORK

1 PREPARE THE VEGETABLES AND ORIENTAL SEASONING

2 PREPARE THE PAPER CASES

3 FILL AND BAKE THE PAPER CASES

1 PREPARE THE VEGETABLES AND ORIENTAL SEASONING

1 Trim the stalk end from each mangetout and pull the string down the pod. Trim the other end.

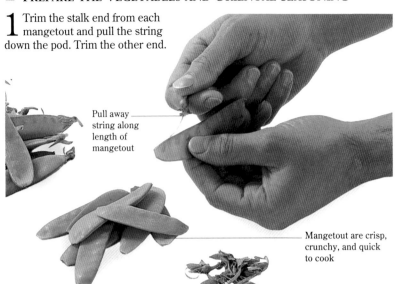

Pull away string along length of mangetout

Mangetout are crisp, crunchy, and quick to cook

2 Half-fill the saucepan with salted water and bring to a boil. Add the mangetout and simmer 1–2 minutes. Drain in the colander, rinse with cold water, and drain again.

3 With the small knife, peel the skin from the root ginger. With the chef's knife, slice the ginger, cutting across the fibrous grain. Crush the slices of ginger with the flat of the knife, then finely chop them.

4 Peel and chop the garlic: set the flat side of the chef's knife on top of each garlic clove and strike it with your fist. Discard the skin and finely chop the garlic.

5 Trim the spring onions. Cut them into thin diagonal slices, including some of the green tops.

Sesame oil is essential flavour in oriental seasoning

6 Put the black fermented beans in the sieve, rinse with cold water, and drain thoroughly. Reserve one-quarter of the whole beans and coarsely chop the rest.

7 Combine the garlic, ginger, chopped and whole black beans, soy sauce, sherry, sugar, and sesame oil in a bowl. Stir the oriental seasoning well to mix, then set aside.

2 PREPARE THE PAPER CASES

1 Fold a sheet of parchment paper (about 30 x 34.5 cm/12 x 15 inches) in half and draw a curve with the pencil to make a heart shape when unfolded. It should be large enough to leave a 7.5 cm (3 inch) border around a fish fillet.

2 Cut out the heart shape with the scissors, cutting just inside the drawn pencil line. Repeat to make a total of 4 paper hearts. Open out each paper heart and brush with the vegetable oil, leaving a border about 2.5 cm (1 inch) wide.

3 For the egg glaze, put the egg and salt in a small bowl and beat with a fork until mixed together. Brush the egg glaze evenly on the border of each of the paper hearts.

3 FILL AND BAKE THE PAPER CASES

Spring onions will keep their crispness when cooked inside paper case

1 Heat the oven to 200°C (400°F, Gas 6). Rinse the fish fillets and pat dry with paper towels. Arrange one-quarter of the mangetout on one side of each paper heart and set a fillet on top.

2 Spoon one-quarter of the oriental seasoning on top of each fillet and sprinkle with one-quarter of the spring onions.

3 Fold the paper over the fish and run your finger along the edge to stick the 2 sides of each paper heart together. Make small pleats to seal the edges of each paper case.

4 Twist the "tails" of each paper case to seal them so that the filling does not ooze out during baking.

Steam from cooked fish puffs paper packages

5 Lay the paper cases on the baking sheet. Bake them in the heated oven until puffed and brown, 10–12 minutes.

🍽 TO SERVE

Transfer the puffed paper cases to warmed individual plates, so that each person can open a paper case. If the paper cases cool and deflate before serving, warm them briefly in the oven to puff them again.

Paper cases enclose wonderful aromas

VARIATION

THAI-STYLE HALIBUT IN A PAPER CASE

1 Omit the mangetout and the oriental seasoning.

2 Put 20 g (³/₄ oz) dried Chinese black mushrooms in a bowl of warm water and soak until plump, about 30 minutes. Drain and slice if large.

3 Finely chop the fresh root ginger and 2 garlic cloves as directed. Slice 2 spring onions.

4 Cut 1 fresh green chilli lengthwise in half, discarding the core. Scrape out the seeds and cut away the fleshy white ribs from each half. Cut each half into very thin strips, then cut across to produce very fine dice.

5 Strip the leaves from 5 sprigs of fresh basil. Peel and slice 1 lime. Squeeze the juice from a second lime.

6 Put the mushrooms, chopped garlic, 15 ml (1 tbsp) soy sauce, 5 ml (1 tsp) sugar, and 125 ml (4 fl oz) water in a small saucepan and boil until all the liquid has evaporated, 5–7 minutes. Stir in the ginger, chilli, basil leaves, 10 ml (2 tsp) fish sauce (nam pla), and the lime juice.

7 Prepare the paper cases and fish as directed. Set the fish on the paper cases, spoon over the mushroom mixture, then sprinkle with the spring onions. Put a lime slice on top and season with pepper. Close the paper cases and bake in the heated oven as directed.

8 If you like, accompany each serving with a fine ribbon pasta, decorated with shredded basil and diced mushroom.

TUNA AND BACON KEBABS

🍽 SERVES 8   🥣 WORK TIME 20–25 MINUTES*   ♨ GRILLING TIME 10–12 MINUTES

EQUIPMENT

whisk

small knife

pastry brush

chef's knife

colander

paper towels

8 long metal skewers

bowls

chopping board

ANNE SAYS
"You could use bamboo skewers, instead of the metal ones suggested here, but cover them with water and soak 30 minutes first."

Chunks of tuna are steeped in a tart marinade, then wrapped in rashers of bacon and threaded onto skewers with cherry tomatoes to be quickly grilled. A salad of spinach and mango creates a tropical presentation.

GETTING AHEAD

The tuna can be marinated and the salad and dressing prepared up to 4 hours ahead; keep the fish and salad in the refrigerator. Assemble and grill the kebabs and toss the salad just before serving.

* plus 30–60 minutes marinating time

INGREDIENTS

tuna fillet †

streaky bacon

cherry tomatoes

vegetable oil

spinach leaves

Dijon mustard

lime juice

olive oil

mango

Tabasco sauce

† other suitable fish
swordfish

metric	SHOPPING LIST	imperial
1.2 kg	skinned tuna fillet or steak	2½ lb
500 g	cherry tomatoes	1 lb
500 g	streaky bacon rashers	1 lb
	vegetable oil for skewers and grill rack	
	salt and pepper	
	For the marinade	
75 ml	lime juice, from 2 limes	2½ fl oz
30 ml	olive oil	2 tbsp
	Tabasco sauce	
	For the spinach and mango salad	
250 g	spinach leaves	8 oz
1	ripe mango	1
	juice of 1 lime	
1.25 ml	Dijon mustard	¼ tsp
75 ml	vegetable oil	2½ fl oz

ORDER OF WORK

1 PREPARE AND MARINATE THE TUNA

2 PREPARE THE SALAD AND DRESSING

3 ASSEMBLE AND GRILL THE KEBABS; TOSS THE SALAD

PREPARE AND MARINATE THE TUNA

1 Rinse the tuna with cold water and pat dry with paper towels. Cut the fish lengthwise into 4 cm (1¹/₂ inch) strips, then cut the strips crosswise into cubes.

Slice tuna into strips first to make neat cubes

Cut strips into even chunks, so they cook at same speed

2 Make the marinade: whisk the lime juice with the olive oil, a dash of Tabasco sauce, and a little salt and pepper in a large non-metallic bowl.

3 Add the cubes of tuna and toss until they are well coated with the marinade. Cover and marinate 30–60 minutes in the refrigerator.

PREPARE THE SALAD AND DRESSING

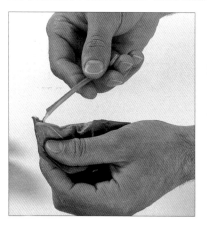

1 Remove the tough ribs and stalks from the spinach leaves, pulling them away with your fingers.

2 Wash the spinach leaves thoroughly and pat dry in a tea towel.

Blot all water from spinach leaves

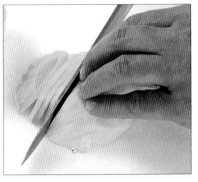

3 Peel the mango with the small knife. Cut lengthwise into 2 pieces, slightly off centre so the knife just misses the stone. Cut the flesh away from the other side of the stone.

4 Cut the pieces of mango flesh into neat slices. Cut the remaining mango flesh away from the stone and neatly slice, then discard the stone.

5 Make the dressing: in a small bowl whisk the lime juice with the mustard, salt, and pepper. Gradually whisk in the oil so the dressing emulsifies. Taste for seasoning.

3 ASSEMBLE AND GRILL THE KEBABS; TOSS THE SALAD

1 Put the cherry tomatoes in the colander and rinse under cold running water. Transfer the tomatoes to paper towels to dry.

Spread out cherry tomatoes on paper towels so they will be dry before grilling

2 Cut the bacon rashers crosswise in half. Each piece should be about 6 cm (2½ inches) long. Heat the grill. Brush the metal skewers and the grill rack with oil.

Bacon wrapping helps keep tuna moist and juicy

3 Wrap a piece of bacon around each cube of tuna. Thread the bacon-wrapped fish onto the skewers, alternating the fish with the cherry tomatoes.

! TAKE CARE !
Do not pack the ingredients too tightly on the skewers or they will not cook evenly.

4 Set the assembled kebabs on the prepared grill rack, in 2 batches if necessary, and grill the kebabs about 7.5 cm (3 inches) from the heat until the bacon is crisp and golden, 5–6 minutes. Turn the kebabs and continue grilling until the fish is cooked through, 5–6 minutes longer.

Arrange mango slices attractively

5 Meanwhile, toss the spinach leaves with three-quarters of the dressing. Spread the spinach on 8 individual plates and arrange the mango slices on top. Sprinkle with the remaining dressing.

🍽 **TO SERVE**
Place a grilled tuna and bacon kebab across the centre of the spinach leaves on each plate.

Bacon is a crisp and tasty wrapping for tuna cubes

Spinach makes a tender bed for kebabs

VARIATION
MONKFISH AND BACON KEBABS

Chunks of monkfish wrapped in bacon alternate with purple-red onions to make up the kebabs.

1 Replace the tuna with the same weight of monkfish fillet. Cut away the thin membrane covering the outside of the monkfish, then cut the fish into cubes and marinate as directed.
2 Prepare the spinach and dressing as directed; omit the mango.
3 Clean, trim, and thinly slice 125 g (4 oz) mushrooms.
4 Cut 2 avocados in half, discard the stones, and peel off the skin. Cut the avocado halves lengthwise into strips and sprinkle them thoroughly with the juice of 1 lime.
5 Peel 4 small purple-red onions and cut each into wedges, leaving a little of the root to hold each wedge together.
6 Wrap the monkfish cubes in bacon and thread them onto the skewers, alternating with the onion wedges. Grill the kebabs as directed.
7 Meanwhile, toss the spinach in three-quarters of the dressing, arrange on individual plates, and top with the mushroom slices and avocado strips. Sprinkle with the remaining dressing.
8 Slide the bacon-wrapped fish and the onions off the skewers and arrange on the salad. Serve immediately.

NEW ENGLAND COD AND MUSSEL CHOWDER

🍽️ SERVES 8 🥣 WORK TIME 45–50 MINUTES 🍲 COOKING TIME 55–60 MINUTES

EQUIPMENT

small knife

chef's knife

stiff brush

large saucepan

colander   vegetable peeler

wooden spoon

paper towels

bowls

large casserole

chopping board

INGREDIENTS

cod fillets †

mussels

potatoes

fresh dill

onions

celery

bay leaves   streaky bacon rashers

carrot   plain flour

dried thyme

double cream

white wine

fish stock

† other suitable fish
haddock, hake, pollack

This hearty American fish stew is laden with chunks of cod and potatoes, with mussels in their shells to add colour and flavour. At the end of cooking, some of the potatoes are crushed to thicken the chowder. Oyster crackers are the traditional accompaniment.

GETTING AHEAD

The chowder can be made up to and including step 7 up to 2 days ahead and kept, covered, in the refrigerator. Finish the chowder just before serving.

metric	SHOPPING LIST	imperial
2	medium onions	2
2	sticks of celery	2
1	medium carrot	1
3	medium potatoes, total weight about 500 g (1 lb)	3
5–7	sprigs of fresh dill	5–7
175 g	streaky bacon rashers	6 oz
1 kg	skinned cod fillets	2 lb
1 kg	mussels	2 lb
1.5 litres	fish stock (see box, page 124)	2¹/₂ pints
2	bay leaves	2
125 ml	white wine	4 fl oz
10 ml	dried thyme	2 tsp
60 g	plain flour	2 oz
250 ml	double cream	8 fl oz
	salt and pepper	

ORDER OF WORK

1 PREPARE THE CHOWDER INGREDIENTS

2 MAKE THE CHOWDER

1 PREPARE THE CHOWDER INGREDIENTS

1 Peel the onions, leaving a little of the root attached, and cut them in half through root and stalk. Slice each half horizontally towards the root, leaving the slices attached at the root end, then slice vertically, again leaving the root end uncut. Finally, cut across the onion to make dice.

Crunchy celery will become soft and tender when simmered

Remove tough celery strings with vegetable peeler

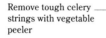

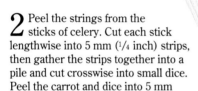

2 Peel the strings from the sticks of celery. Cut each stick lengthwise into 5 mm (¼ inch) strips, then gather the strips together into a pile and cut crosswise into small dice. Peel the carrot and dice into 5 mm (¼ inch) cubes (see box, below).

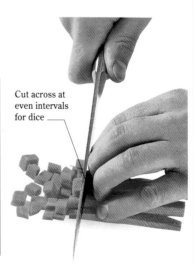

HOW TO DICE VEGETABLES

Root vegetables, such as carrots, turnips, and potatoes, are often diced before cooking. The size of the dice depends on the thickness of the initial slices.

Cut across at even intervals for dice

1 After peeling or trimming the vegetable, if necessary square off the sides, using a chef's knife to achieve a neat finish.

2 Cut the vegetable vertically into slices of the specified thickness. Stack the slices on the chopping board and cut them into strips of the specified thickness.

3 Gather the strips together into a pile and cut them crosswise to produce even dice.

Cold water prevents diced potatoes from discolouring

3 Peel and dice potatoes into 1 cm (^{1}/$_2$ inch) cubes (see box, page 35). Put in a bowl of cold water so they do not discolour.

4 Strip the dill leaves from the stalks and pile them on the chopping board. With the chef's knife, coarsely chop the leaves and set aside for decoration of the finished dish.

5 Stack the bacon rashers on the chopping board and cut across into strips, then chop the strips into dice.

6 Rinse the cod fillets thoroughly with cold water and pat dry with paper towels. Remove any bones and cut the fillets into 2.5 cm (1 inch) strips, then cut them across into 2.5 cm (1 inch) cubes. Prepare the mussels (see box, page 37).

Cubes of cod will cook quickly

To simplify cutting up cod, slice it first into strips, then across into pieces

HOW TO PREPARE MUSSELS

Before cooking, mussels must be carefully scraped and washed to remove barnacles, sand, and the "beard" that attaches them to the poles or ropes on which cultivated mussels grow.

1 With a small knife, detach and discard any weed or "beard" from the mussels. Scrape each mussel to remove any barnacles.

! TAKE CARE !
Discard any mussels that have broken shells or that do not close when tapped.

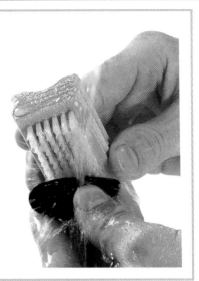

2 Scrub the mussels thoroughly under cold running water using a stiff brush.

MAKE THE CHOWDER

White wine adds acidity to chowder

1 Put the fish stock and bay leaves in the pan and pour in the wine. Heat the stock mixture to boiling and simmer 10 minutes.

! TAKE CARE !
Do not simmer fish stock too long, or it will be bitter.

2 Meanwhile, put the bacon in the casserole and cook, stirring occasionally, until crisp and the fat is rendered (melted), 3–5 minutes.

3 Add the diced onions, celery, carrot, and thyme. Cook, stirring, until the vegetables are soft but not brown, 5–7 minutes.

Aromatic bay leaves give depth of flavour to chowder

4 Sprinkle the flour over the bacon and vegetables in the casserole and cook, stirring, 1 minute.

Flour helps to thicken chowder

Stir to distribute flour evenly

5 Add the hot stock mixture to the vegetables and bring to a boil, stirring until the liquid boils and thickens slightly.

6 Drain the potatoes and add them to the casserole. Simmer, stirring occasionally, until the potatoes are very tender, about 40 minutes.

7 Remove the casserole from the heat. Using a fork, crush about one-third of the potatoes against the side of the casserole, then stir to combine.

ANNE SAYS
"The crushed potatoes help thicken the chowder."

Tip in cleaned mussels all at once

Mussels will open quickly in heat of chowder

8 Return the casserole to the heat. Add the mussels to the chowder and simmer until the shells start to open, 1–2 minutes.

9 Stir in the cubed cod and simmer the chowder until the fish just flakes easily, 2–3 minutes longer.

10 Pour in the double cream and bring just to a boil. Taste the chowder for seasoning.

🍽 **TO SERVE**
Discard the bay leaves and any mussels that have not opened. Ladle the chowder into soup bowls and sprinkle each serving with the chopped dill. Serve very hot, with oyster crackers to scatter over the stew.

Creamy chowder is deliciously rich and satisfying

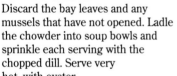

VARIATION

MANHATTAN COD AND MUSSEL CHOWDER

Manhattan chowder adds tomatoes, tomato purée, and thyme for a colourful finish.

1 Prepare the chowder ingredients as directed in the main recipe.
2 Cut the cores from 1.2 kg (2½ lb) tomatoes and score an "x" on the base of each with the tip of a knife. Immerse them in a pan of boiling water until the skin starts to split, 8–15 seconds depending on their ripeness. Using a slotted spoon, transfer at once to cold water. When cold, peel off the skins. Cut the tomatoes crosswise in half and squeeze out the seeds, then coarsely chop each half. Alternatively, use 750 ml (1¼ pints) canned tomatoes.
3 Peel 4 garlic cloves: set the flat side of the chef's knife on top of each clove and strike it with your fist. Discard the skin and finely chop the garlic.
4 Make the chowder as directed, using double the amount of white wine, 15 ml (1 tbsp) dried thyme, and half the amount of plain flour. Add the garlic and 15–30 ml (1–2 tbsp) tomato purée with the onions, celery, and carrots. Add the chopped tomatoes with the potatoes; do not crush any of the potatoes. Omit the double cream.
5 Sprinkle with chopped thyme and serve the chowder with crusty whole wheat bread, if you like.

PERFECT FISH AND CHIPS

 SERVES 4 WORK TIME 45–50 MINUTES* DEEP-FRYING TIME 20–25 MINUTES

EQUIPMENT

deep-fat fryer with thermostat

wooden spoon

vegetable peeler   small knife

bowls

chef's knife

whisk †

2-pronged fork

baking tray   chopping board

paper towels

colander

† electric mixer can also be used

ANNE SAYS

"If you have no thermostat with your fryer, drop in a cube of fresh bread to test the temperature; if it turns golden in 60 seconds, the oil is about 180°C (350°F), if it is golden in 40 seconds the oil is about 190°C (375°F)."

This time-honoured favourite features cod deep-fried in a light beer batter. For crispness, the chips are deep-fried twice: first to cook them, then to brown them. The traditional accompaniment is tartare sauce.

GETTING AHEAD

The fish and batter can be prepared, and the chips given one deep-frying, up to 2 hours ahead. Deep-fry the fish and brown the chips just before serving so they will be crisp.

plus 30–35 minutes standing time

metric	SHOPPING LIST	imperial
6	potatoes, total weight about 750 g (1½ lb)	6
	vegetable oil for deep-frying	
750 g	skinned cod fillets	1½ lb
1	lemon	1
30 g	plain flour	1 oz
	salt and pepper	
	For the batter	
7.5 ml	dried yeast (or 9 g/⅓ oz fresh yeast)	1½ tsp
60 ml	warm water	4 tbsp
150 g	plain flour	5 oz
15 ml	vegetable oil	1 tbsp
175 ml	bitter ale	6 fl oz
1	egg white	1
	tartare sauce (see box, page 43) for serving (optional)	

INGREDIENTS

cod fillets †

lemon

vegetable oil

potatoes

egg white

oil for deep-frying

bitter ale ‡

dried yeast

plain flour

†other suitable fish
haddock, hake, hoki, huss, plaice

‡ light ale or lager can also be used

ORDER OF WORK

1. **PREPARE THE POTATOES AND BATTER**

2. **PART-FRY THE CHIPS AND PREPARE THE FISH**

3. **COAT AND DEEP-FRY THE FISH; BROWN THE CHIPS**

1 PREPARE THE POTATOES AND BATTER

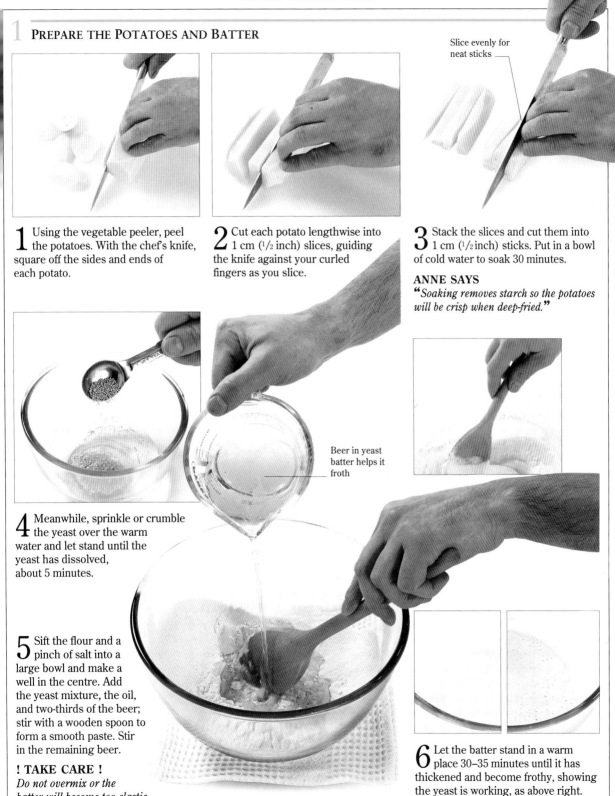

Slice evenly for
neat sticks

1 Using the vegetable peeler, peel the potatoes. With the chef's knife, square off the sides and ends of each potato.

2 Cut each potato lengthwise into 1 cm (1/2 inch) slices, guiding the knife against your curled fingers as you slice.

3 Stack the slices and cut them into 1 cm (1/2 inch) sticks. Put in a bowl of cold water to soak 30 minutes.

ANNE SAYS
"Soaking removes starch so the potatoes will be crisp when deep-fried."

Beer in yeast
batter helps it
froth

4 Meanwhile, sprinkle or crumble the yeast over the warm water and let stand until the yeast has dissolved, about 5 minutes.

5 Sift the flour and a pinch of salt into a large bowl and make a well in the centre. Add the yeast mixture, the oil, and two-thirds of the beer; stir with a wooden spoon to form a smooth paste. Stir in the remaining beer.

! TAKE CARE !
Do not overmix or the batter will become too elastic.

6 Let the batter stand in a warm place 30–35 minutes until it has thickened and become frothy, showing the yeast is working, as above right.

PART-FRY THE CHIPS AND PREPARE THE FISH

1 While the batter is standing, heat the vegetable oil in the deep-fat fryer to 180°C (350°F). Drain the potatoes, transfer to paper towels, and pat dry.

Dry potatoes thoroughly: any water left on them will make hot oil spit

2 Dip the empty frying basket in the hot oil (this will prevent the potatoes from sticking to it). Lift the basket out of the oil and add the potatoes. Carefully lower the basket back into the oil and deep-fry until the potatoes are just tender when pierced with the tip of the small knife, and are just starting to brown, 5–7 minutes. Lift out the basket and let the potatoes drain over the deep fryer, then tip them onto a plate lined with paper towels.

! TAKE CARE !
Do not overfill the basket or the oil could bubble over. Deep-fry the potatoes in batches if necessary.

After first deep-frying, potatoes should be just tender

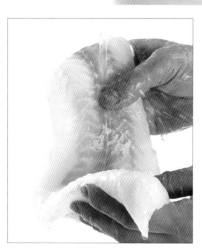

3 Rinse the fish fillets under cold running water and pat dry with paper towels.

4 Divide the fish into 4 portions, cutting neatly on the diagonal with the chef's knife. Cut the lemon in half, then cut each lemon half into even-sized wedges. Set aside for decoration.

TARTARE SAUCE

This classic accompaniment adds piquancy to the richness of deep-fried fish. Here the ingredients are roughly chopped, then bound together with creamy mayonnaise. The sauce can be made up to 2 days ahead and kept, covered, in the refrigerator.

🍴 SERVES 4

🥣 WORK TIME 20–25 MINUTES

SHOPPING LIST

1	hard-boiled egg	1
2	gherkins	2
5 ml	drained capers	1 tsp
1	small shallot	1
2–3	sprigs of parsley	2–3
2–3	sprigs of fresh chervil or tarragon	2–3
125 ml	bottled mayonnaise	4 fl oz
	salt and pepper	

Coarsely chop ingredients for tartare sauce to add texture

Gherkins give sauce refreshing tang

1 Tap the egg to crack the shell. Shell it and rinse with cold water. Coarsely chop the egg.

2 With a chef's knife, coarsely chop the gherkins, then chop the capers.

3 Peel and halve the shallot; set it flat-side down on a chopping board. Slice horizontally towards the root, leaving the slices attached at the root. Slice vertically, again leaving the root end uncut, and cut across the shallot to make fine dice.

4 Strip the parsley leaves and chervil or tarragon leaves from the stalks and pile them on the chopping board. Using a chef's knife, hold the tip of the blade against the board and rock the blade back and forth to coarsely chop the herb leaves.

Fold lightly so ingredients are not crushed

5 Mix together the mayonnaise, chopped egg, capers, gherkins, shallot, and herbs and taste for seasoning. Cover and refrigerate until serving.

3 COAT AND DEEP-FRY THE FISH; BROWN THE CHIPS

Whites gather in whisk wires when stiff

1 Heat the oven to low. Heat the oil to 190°C (375°F). Put the flour on a plate and season with salt and pepper. Coat the pieces of fish with the seasoned flour, patting with your hands so they are evenly coated.

For maximum volume, use circular motion when whisking

2 Beat the egg white in a medium metal bowl until stiff peaks form when the whisk is lifted.

3 Gently fold the whisked egg white into the batter, using the wooden spoon, until combined.

4 Using the 2-pronged fork, dip a piece of fish in the batter, turning to coat thoroughly. Lift out the fish and hold it over the bowl 5 seconds so excess batter can drip off.

5 Carefully lower the piece of fish into the hot oil and deep-fry, turning once, until golden brown and crisp, 6–8 minutes depending on the thickness of the fish. Coat and deep-fry the remaining fish, 1 or 2 pieces at a time.

ANNE SAYS
"*Remove any scraps of batter from the oil in between batches.*"

Using 2-pronged fork, lower piece of fish gently into hot oil so oil does not bubble up too much

6 As the fish is deep-fried, transfer to the baking tray lined with paper towels so that excess oil is absorbed. Keep warm in the oven.

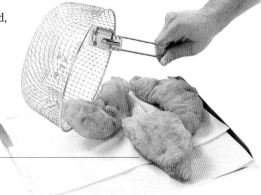

Paper towels absorb excess fat so batter-fried fish remain crisp

Chips remain crisp if salt is not sprinkled on until just before serving

7 Put the partially cooked chips in the frying basket and deep-fry until very hot and golden brown, 1–2 minutes. Drain on paper towels.

🍽 **TO SERVE**

Divide the fish and chips among warmed individual plates. Sprinkle the chips with a little salt. Decorate the fish with the lemon wedges and serve at once, accompanied by tartare sauce, if you like.

VARIATION

TEMPURA-STYLE FISH WITH SWEET POTATOES

A light tempura batter coats this fish, which is served with a Japanese-style dipping sauce.

1 Make the dipping sauce: finely grate about 60 g (2 oz) mooli (daikon or white radish). With a small knife, peel the skin from a 2.5 cm (1 inch) piece of fresh root ginger. Slice the ginger, cutting across the grain, then crush each slice with the flat of a chef's knife and finely chop. Mix together 125 ml (4 fl oz) each of sake (rice wine) and light soy sauce, then add the grated mooli, root ginger, and 5 ml (1 tsp) sugar, or more to taste. Set aside.

2 Make the batter: sift 250 g (8 oz) plain flour. Lightly beat 2 eggs in a large shallow bowl and stir in 500 ml (16 fl oz) cold water. Add the flour all at once and mix just until combined; the consistency should be lumpy.

3 Heat the vegetable oil to 190°C (375°F). Peel 2 sweet potatoes (total weight about 375 g/12 oz), halve length-wise, and cut into 5 mm ($^{1}/_{4}$ inch) slices; it is not necessary to soak them.

4 Coat the sweet potatoes in seasoned flour, then in the batter, and deep-fry until tender and golden, 4–6 minutes; drain and keep warm in a low oven.

5 Rinse and pat dry the fish, then divide into 4 portions, as directed. Coat the fish in the seasoned flour and batter and deep-fry as directed.

6 Serve the fish with the sweet potatoes and dipping sauce. Decorate with fresh chive stalks, omitting the lemon wedges.

FISHERMAN'S PIE

🍽 SERVES 6 🥄 WORK TIME 35–45 MINUTES 🍲 BAKING TIME 20–30 MINUTES

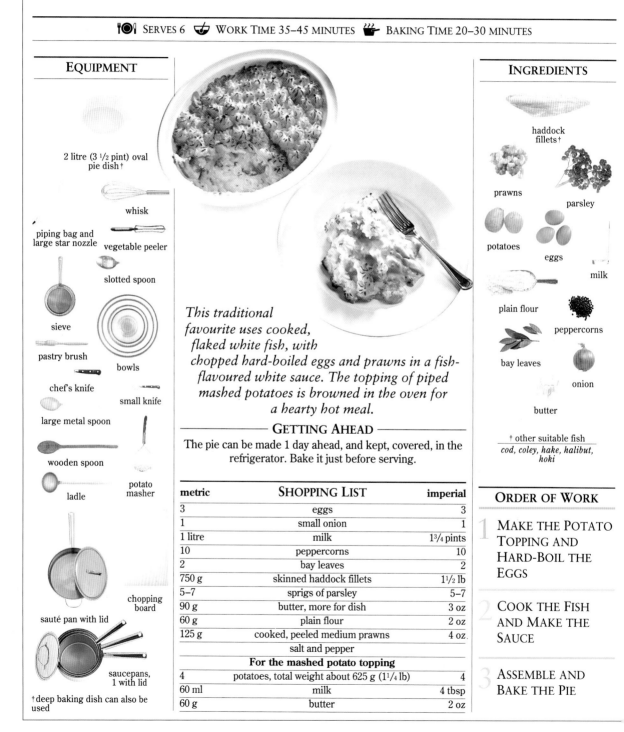

EQUIPMENT

2 litre (3 ½ pint) oval pie dish†

whisk

piping bag and large star nozzle

vegetable peeler

slotted spoon

sieve

pastry brush

bowls

chef's knife

small knife

large metal spoon

wooden spoon

potato masher

ladle

chopping board

sauté pan with lid

saucepans, 1 with lid

†deep baking dish can also be used

INGREDIENTS

haddock fillets†

prawns

parsley

potatoes

eggs

milk

plain flour

peppercorns

bay leaves

onion

butter

† other suitable fish
cod, coley, hake, halibut, hoki

This traditional favourite uses cooked, flaked white fish, with chopped hard-boiled eggs and prawns in a fish-flavoured white sauce. The topping of piped mashed potatoes is browned in the oven for a hearty hot meal.

GETTING AHEAD

The pie can be made 1 day ahead, and kept, covered, in the refrigerator. Bake it just before serving.

metric	SHOPPING LIST	imperial
3	eggs	3
1	small onion	1
1 litre	milk	1¾ pints
10	peppercorns	10
2	bay leaves	2
750 g	skinned haddock fillets	1½ lb
5–7	sprigs of parsley	5–7
90 g	butter, more for dish	3 oz
60 g	plain flour	2 oz
125 g	cooked, peeled medium prawns	4 oz
	salt and pepper	
For the mashed potato topping		
4	potatoes, total weight about 625 g (1¼ lb)	4
60 ml	milk	4 tbsp
60 g	butter	2 oz

ORDER OF WORK

1 MAKE THE POTATO TOPPING AND HARD-BOIL THE EGGS

2 COOK THE FISH AND MAKE THE SAUCE

3 ASSEMBLE AND BAKE THE PIE

MAKE THE POTATO TOPPING AND HARD-BOIL THE EGGS

1 Wash and peel the potatoes. Cut them into pieces. Half-fill a medium saucepan with water, add salt, then the potatoes, and bring to a boil.

2 Simmer the potatoes until tender when pierced with the tip of the small knife, 15–20 minutes. Meanwhile, hard-boil and shell the eggs (see box, page 48).

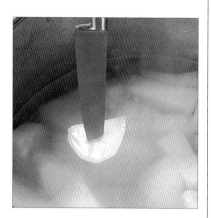

Thoroughly cooked potatoes mash easily

3 Drain the potatoes thoroughly. Using the potato masher, mash the potatoes in the saucepan.

4 Heat the milk in a small saucepan. Add the butter, salt, and pepper to the milk and stir until mixed. Pour the hot milk mixture into the potatoes.

Fold piping bag over hand for support while filling with mashed potato

6 Let the potatoes cool slightly, then spoon them into the piping bag fitted with the star nozzle. Set aside.

5 Beat the mixture constantly over medium heat until the potatoes are light and fluffy, about 5 minutes. Taste the potatoes for seasoning.

Fluffy mashed potato will be easy to pipe

HOW TO HARD-BOIL AND SHELL EGGS

1 Put the eggs in a medium saucepan of cold water. Bring the water to a boil and simmer the eggs, 10 minutes.

2 Remove the pan from the heat and immediately run cold water into the pan to stop the eggs cooking. Allow the eggs to cool in the water.

3 Drain the eggs. Tap gently to crack the shells all over, then remove the shells. Rinse the eggs and dry with paper towels.

COOK THE FISH AND MAKE THE SAUCE

1 Peel and quarter the onion. Pour the milk into the sauté pan, then add the peppercorns, bay leaves, and onion quarters to the milk.

2 Bring the milk mixture to a boil, then remove from the heat. Cover the sauté pan and let stand in a warm place to infuse, about 10 minutes.

Milk infused with
flavourings makes
aromatic cooking
liquid for fish

4 Add the fish to the milk mixture, cover the pan, and simmer until the fish flakes easily when tested with a fork, 5–10 minutes, depending on the thickness of the fillets.

Fish pieces
will cook quickly

3 With the chef's knife, cut each of the fillets across into pieces.

6 Strip the parsley leaves from the stalks and pile them on the chopping board. With the chef's knife, coarsely chop the parsley leaves.

Pinch off leaves from stalks with fingers

Parsley will add fresh flavour to sauce

5 Transfer the fish to a large plate, using the slotted spoon; reserve the cooking liquid. Let the fish cool, then flake with a fork.

ANNE SAYS
"To find any leftover bones, pick over the fish with your fingers."

7 To make the sauce, gently melt the butter in a medium saucepan over medium heat. Whisk in the flour and cook until foaming, 30–60 seconds.

8 Remove the butter and flour mixture from the heat. Pour the reserved fish cooking liquid through the sieve into the butter and flour mixture.

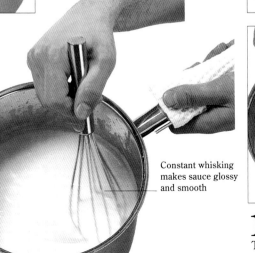

9 Whisk the liquid into the sauce, then return to the heat, and cook, whisking constantly, until the sauce boils and thickens. Season with salt and pepper and simmer 2 minutes.

! TAKE CARE !
If the sauce forms lumps at any stage, stop heating and whisk vigorously. If this is not sufficient, strain the sauce.

Constant whisking makes sauce glossy and smooth

10 Stir the chopped parsley into the sauce, using the whisk. Taste for seasoning.

3 ASSEMBLE AND BAKE THE PIE

1 Heat the oven to 180°C (350°F, Gas 4). Melt some butter and butter the pie dish.

2 Set the hard-boiled eggs on the chopping board and chop them coarsely with the chef's knife.

Grip egg with fingertips as you chop

3 Ladle one-third of the sauce into the bottom of the pie dish.

4 Spoon the flaked haddock on top of the sauce, distributing the fish in an even layer.

Hard-boiled eggs add body and texture to pie

5 Cover the fish with the remaining sauce, then distribute the prawns evenly on the surface.

Arrange prawns on sauce

6 Sprinkle the chopped hard-boiled eggs over the top of the prawns.

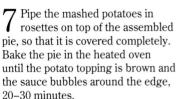

7 Pipe the mashed potatoes in rosettes on top of the assembled pie, so that it is covered completely. Bake the pie in the heated oven until the potato topping is brown and the sauce bubbles around the edge, 20–30 minutes.

ANNE SAYS

"*Alternatively, spread the mashed potatoes over the top of the pie, making peaks with a fork.*"

Be sure eggs and prawns are completely covered with potato rosettes

|⦿| TO SERVE

Serve the pie hot from the pie dish, onto warmed individual plates.

Piped potato rosettes are an appealing topping

Pie filling is moist and richly flavoured with a delicious combination of fish and prawns

INDIVIDUAL FISH CRUMBLES

In this recipe rolled oats are combined with chopped parsley and grated Parmesan cheese to add texture.

1 Follow the main recipe, replacing the potato topping with crumble topping: sift 150 g (5 oz) plain flour into a medium bowl. Using 2 table knives, cut 90 g (3 oz) butter into small pieces in the flour.

2 With your fingertips, rub the pieces of butter into the flour until the mixture resembles fine crumbs. Alternatively, blend the butter with the flour in a food processor.

3 Chop the leaves from 3–5 additional sprigs of parsley.

4 Stir 40 g (1½ oz) rolled oats into the blended butter and flour, with the additional chopped parsley, 15 ml (1 tbsp) grated Parmesan cheese, salt, and pepper.

5 Butter 6 individual casserole dishes and layer the ingredients as directed in the main recipe, dividing them equally among the casserole dishes.

6 Sprinkle the oat crumble topping over the pie filling in each dish, and bake 20–25 minutes.

7 If necessary, brown the individual fish crumbles under the grill, 1–2 minutes.

SALTIMBOCCA OF SALMON

 SERVES 4–6 WORK TIME 20–25 MINUTES* COOKING TIME 1–2 MINUTES

EQUIPMENT

shallow non-metallic dish

palette knife

chef's knife

filleting knife

small knife

large frying pan

slotted spoon

saucepan

paper towels

tweezers

bowls

wooden cocktail sticks

metal skewer

cling film

chopping board

Chef Chambrette, a legend at La Varenne cooking school, introduced me to this variation on traditional saltimbocca of veal. Slices of salmon are marinated in olive oil and herbs, wrapped around smoked salmon, and sautéed. A light tomato-basil garnish is the finishing touch.

GETTING AHEAD

The salmon slices can be marinated and rolled up to 4 hours ahead and kept refrigerated. They should be sautéed just before serving.

*plus 1¹/₂–2 hours marinating time

INGREDIENTS

fresh salmon fillet†

 olive oil

sliced smoked salmon

lemon juice

fresh basil

 bay leaves

granulated sugar

tomatoes   butter

fresh thyme

† other suitable fish
bass

metric	SHOPPING LIST	imperial
1 kg	fresh salmon fillet, with its skin	2 lb
5–7	sprigs of fresh basil	5–7
250 g	sliced smoked salmon	8 oz
45 g	butter	1¹/₂ oz
	salt and pepper	
	For the marinade	
	juice of ¹/₂ lemon	
175 ml	olive oil	6 fl oz
3–4	sprigs of fresh thyme	3–4
2	bay leaves	2
	For the tomato-basil garnish	
4	tomatoes, total weight about 625 g (1¹/₄ lb)	4
1	small bunch of fresh basil	1
30 ml	olive oil	2 tbsp
1	pinch of granulated sugar	1

ORDER OF WORK

1 PREPARE AND MARINATE THE FRESH SALMON SLICES

2 MAKE THE TOMATO-BASIL GARNISH

3 ROLL AND COOK THE SALTIMBOCCA

1 PREPARE AND MARINATE THE FRESH SALMON SLICES

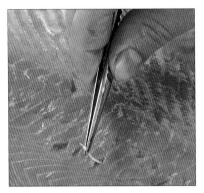

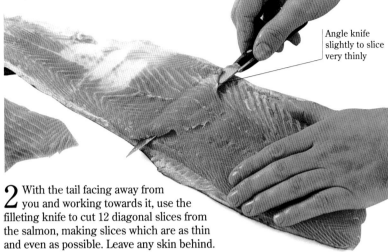

Angle knife slightly to slice very thinly

1 Rinse the salmon fillet with cold water and pat dry with paper towels. If necessary, cut out the remnants of the central bone and pull out any pin bones with the tweezers.

2 With the tail facing away from you and working towards it, use the filleting knife to cut 12 diagonal slices from the salmon, making slices which are as thin and even as possible. Leave any skin behind.

3 Make the marinade: put the lemon juice and oil in the shallow dish. Strip the thyme leaves from the stalks and add to the dish with pepper. Crush the bay leaves into the dish.

4 Add the slices of fresh salmon to the marinade. Cover and marinate the slices in the refrigerator, 1 hour. Meanwhile, make the tomato-basil garnish.

2 MAKE THE TOMATO-BASIL GARNISH

Chop basil coarsely to give garnish texture

1 Cut the cores from the tomatoes; score an "x" on the base of each. Immerse in boiling water until the skin starts to split, 8–15 seconds. Transfer to cold water. When cold, peel off the skin. Cut crosswise in half, squeeze out the seeds, then chop.

2 Strip the basil leaves from the stalks and pile them on the chopping board. With the chef's knife, coarsely chop the leaves.

3 Mix the tomatoes with the oil and chopped basil and season to taste with salt, pepper, and a pinch of sugar. Let stand to marinate 30–60 minutes at room temperature.

3 ROLL AND COOK THE SALTIMBOCCA

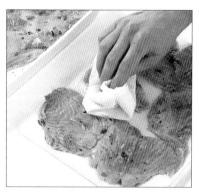

1 Transfer the fresh salmon slices from the marinade to paper towels. Pat dry with paper towels.

2 Strip the basil leaves from the stalks. Cut the smoked salmon slices into pieces the same size as the fresh salmon slices.

Fresh basil gives pungent flavour

Fresh and smoked salmon will make tasty contrast

3 Assemble the saltimbocca: arrange a piece of smoked salmon on top of each of 3 fresh salmon slices. Put a basil leaf in the centre of each piece of smoked salmon.

4 Roll up the assembled saltimbocca. Secure each with a cocktail stick, threading it in and out along the seam.

5 Assemble and roll the remaining fresh salmon slices, pieces of smoked salmon, and basil leaves in the same way.

6 Heat the butter in the frying pan and add a batch of salmon saltimbocca, leaving space around them in the pan.

7 Cook the saltimbocca over high heat, turning them occasionally, until lightly browned on all sides, 1–2 minutes.

! TAKE CARE !
Do not overcook the saltimbocca or they will be dry.

Turn to brown lightly and evenly

8 Test the saltimbocca for tenderness by piercing with a skewer. Remove from the pan and keep them warm while you cook the remaining saltimbocca.

¶◎¶ TO SERVE
Remove the cocktail sticks from the saltimbocca. Arrange them on warmed individual plates and serve at once with the tomato-basil garnish.

Fresh spinach pasta ribbons are a colourful accompaniment to salmon rolls

Tomato-basil garnish is a refreshing complement

VARIATION
PAUPIETTES OF SOLE
Lemon sole fillets take the place of fresh salmon slices in this steamed version of saltimbocca.

1 Make the tomato-basil garnish as directed in the main recipe.
2 Replace the salmon fillet with 6 large skinless fillets of lemon sole (total weight about 500 g/1 lb). Trim the fillets and slice each in half along the central line. Flatten gently with the side of a chef's knife. Omit the marinade.
3 Cut the slices of smoked salmon to fit the pieces of sole.
4 Lay one piece of sole on the work surface, skinned-side up, and put a piece of smoked salmon on top; omit the basil leaf. Starting from the tail end, roll up fairly tightly. (If the roll is very fat, unroll and cut it crosswise in half to make 2 smaller rolls.) Secure with a wooden cocktail stick. Continue making the rest of the rolls.
5 Fill a steamer with 5–7.5 cm (2–3 inches) of water and bring to a boil. Arrange the rolls on the steamer rack, seam-side down, and sprinkle with the juice of 1/2 lemon, salt, and pepper. Set the rack over the simmering water, cover, and cook until tender when pierced with a skewer, 8–10 minutes.
6 Slice and serve with the tomato-basil garnish, decorated with fresh basil.

ROAST MONKFISH WITH GARLIC AND CHILLI SAUCES

 SERVES 6   WORK TIME 25–30 MINUTES*   ROASTING TIME 12–15 MINUTES

EQUIPMENT

shallow glass dish

small saucepan

small knife

pastry brush

chef's knife

food processor

whisk

rubber spatula

paper towels

bowls

chopping board

baking sheet

aluminium foil

rubber gloves

Monkfish is an ugly fish, with a huge head and gaping mouth, but its excellent flesh more than compensates for its disconcerting appearance. These monkfish fillets are roasted whole, then sliced to serve hot or at room temperature with two pungent sauces.

*plus 2 hours marinating time

INGREDIENTS

monkfish fillets†

fresh red chillies

tomato purée

fresh thyme

butter

plain flour

parsley

eggs

olive oil

cayenne pepper

garlic cloves

fresh oregano

† other suitable fish
bass, huss

metric	SHOPPING LIST	imperial
6	skinned monkfish fillets, total weight 1.4 kg (3 lb)	6
5–7	sprigs of fresh oregano	5–7
5–7	sprigs of fresh thyme	5–7
30 ml	olive oil	2 tbsp
	salt and pepper	
	For the garlic and chilli sauces	
4	eggs	4
45 g	butter	1½ oz
45 ml	plain flour	3 tbsp
250 ml	boiling water	8 fl oz
8	garlic cloves, or to taste	8
125 ml	olive oil	4 fl oz
6–9	sprigs of parsley and other fresh herbs such as thyme, oregano, chervil, and tarragon	6–9
2	fresh red chillies	2
10 ml	tomato purée	2 tsp
	cayenne pepper (optional)	

ORDER OF WORK

1 PREPARE AND MARINATE THE MONKFISH

2 MAKE THE SAUCES AND DECORATION

3 ROAST THE MONKFISH

PREPARE AND MARINATE THE MONKFISH

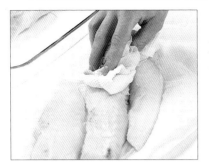

1 If necessary, cut away the thin membrane that covers the flesh of the monkfish fillets. Rinse the fillets with cold water, then transfer to paper towels and pat dry.

2 Strip the oregano and thyme leaves from the stalks and pile them on the chopping board. Roughly chop the leaves.

3 Put the fillets in the shallow dish and sprinkle with the olive oil, chopped herbs, salt, and pepper. Toss with your hands so the fillets are covered with oil. Cover and marinate in the refrigerator 2 hours. Meanwhile, make the sauces.

Lift and turn fillets with your hands

Herb marinade adds flavour to monkfish fillets

MAKE THE SAUCES AND DECORATION

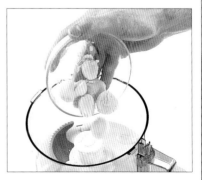

1 Put the eggs in the saucepan, cover with cold water, and bring to a boil. Simmer 10 minutes. Drain the eggs, then let cool in a bowl of cold water. Tap the eggs to crack the shells, then peel them. Separate the yolks from the whites and discard the whites or set them aside for another use.

2 Melt the butter in the saucepan. Whisk in the flour and cook until foaming, about 1 minute. Take from the heat and whisk in the boiling water. The sauce will thicken at once. Return the saucepan to the heat and cook, whisking, 1 minute.

3 Transfer the sauce to the food processor. Peel the garlic cloves. Add to the processor with the hard-boiled egg yolks, salt, and pepper and purée until smooth.

ANNE SAYS
"Add more or less garlic to your taste."

4 With the blades turning, pour in the olive oil in a thin stream, so the sauce thickens and becomes creamy. Taste the sauce for seasoning. Put half of the sauce in a bowl and reserve for the chilli sauce.

! TAKE CARE !
If the oil is added too quickly, the mixture will separate.

5 Strip the parsley and other herb leaves from the stalks and add to the remaining sauce in the processor. Purée briefly. Transfer to a second bowl. Cover and chill until serving.

HOW TO CORE, DESEED, AND CHOP HOT CHILLIES

Be sure to wear rubber gloves and avoid contact with eyes; hot chillies can burn hands and eyes.

1 Cut the chillies lengthwise in half with a small knife. Cut out the core and fleshy white ribs.

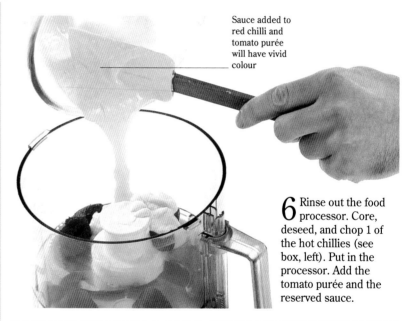

Sauce added to red chilli and tomato purée will have vivid colour

6 Rinse out the food processor. Core, deseed, and chop 1 of the hot chillies (see box, left). Put in the processor. Add the tomato purée and the reserved sauce.

2 Scrape out the seeds with the point of a small knife, then roughly chop the chilli halves.

7 Purée until smooth, scraping the side of the food processor with the rubber spatula. Season with cayenne pepper, if you like. Transfer to a bowl, cover, and chill.

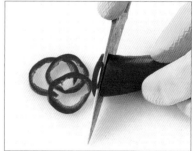

8 Cut out the core from the second chilli and remove the seeds with the tip of the small knife. Cut the chilli into thin rings and reserve for the decoration.

3 ROAST THE MONKFISH

1 Heat the oven to 230°C (450°F, Gas 8). Line the baking sheet with foil. Arrange the monkfish fillets, side by side, on the foil. Spoon the marinade from the dish over the fillets.

Brush makes basting easy during roasting

2 Roast the fillets in the heated oven, brushing occasionally with the juices which have collected on the foil, until browned and the fish is no longer rare in the centre, 12–15 minutes. The flesh should just flake when tested with a fork.

¶◎¶ TO SERVE

Cut the monkfish into diagonal slices. Arrange on warmed individual plates, and add a little of each sauce. Decorate with the rings of chilli, and thyme sprigs if you like. Serve the remaining sauces separately.

Piquant chilli sauce contrasts with sweet flavour of monkfish

VARIATION

GRILLED MONKFISH ESCALOPES WITH GARLIC AND CHILLI SAUCES

Monkfish fillets are cut into thin slices, grilled, and served with these colourful sauces.

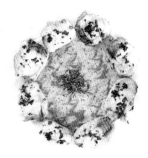

1 Rinse and pat dry the monkfish fillets. Holding each fillet steady with your hand, cut diagonal slices about 1 cm (1/2 inch) thick, working towards the tail and keeping the slices of monkfish as even as possible.
2 Marinate the monkfish slices as directed, using twice the amount of chopped herbs. Meanwhile, make the garlic and chilli sauces as directed. Omit the rings of chilli.
3 Grill the escalopes about 7.5 cm (3 inches) from the heat, 4 minutes; it is not necessary to turn them.
4 Make pools of garlic sauce on warmed individual plates. Drizzle lines of chilli sauce onto each and draw a knife across at even intervals to create a feathered effect. Arrange the fish around the edge of each plate. Decorate with herbs.

Firm flesh of monkfish slices well for presentation

─ GETTING AHEAD ─

The garlic and chilli sauces can be made up to 1 day ahead and kept refrigerated. Roast the monkfish just before serving.

SEAFOOD LASAGNE

🍽 SERVES 8 🥄 WORK TIME 40–45 MINUTES 🍲 BAKING TIME 30–45 MINUTES

EQUIPMENT

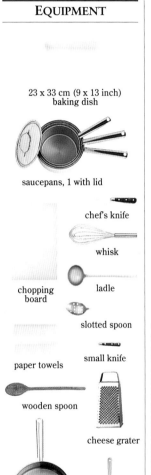

23 x 33 cm (9 x 13 inch)
baking dish

saucepans, 1 with lid

chef's knife

whisk

chopping
board

ladle

slotted spoon

paper towels

small knife

wooden spoon

cheese grater

wide shallow saucepan

sieve

bowls

colander

*This partnership of pasta with seafood, layered
with a rich sauce, is delicious. The seafood is first
lightly sautéed with shallots and white wine, then
the cooking liquid is added to the sauce.*

metric	SHOPPING LIST	imperial
250 g	raw prawns	8 oz
250 g	scallops	8 oz
500 g	lemon sole fillets	1 lb
2	shallots	2
30 g	butter, more for baking dish	1 oz
60 ml	white wine	2 fl oz
15 ml	vegetable oil	1 tbsp
250 g	fresh or dried lasagne noodles	8 oz
90 g	Gruyère cheese	3 oz
	salt and pepper	
	For the sauce	
1	small onion	1
500 ml	milk	16 fl oz
1	bay leaf	1
6	peppercorns	6
500 g	plum tomatoes	1 lb
175 g	mushrooms	6 oz
30 g	butter	1 oz
30 g	plain flour	1 oz
150 ml	double cream	¼ pint
6–8	sprigs of fresh parsley and basil	6–8
1.25 ml	crushed chillies, more to taste	¼ tsp

INGREDIENTS

lemon sole fillets†   raw prawns

lasagne noodles   scallops

white
wine   fresh herbs

double cream   bay leaf

shallots   vegetable
oil

butter

plain flour   mushrooms

Gruyère
cheese   milk   plum
tomatoes

onion   crushed
chillies   peppercorns

† other suitable fish
huss, plaice, red gurnard

ORDER OF WORK

1 PREPARE THE
SEAFOOD

2 MAKE THE SAUCE

3 ASSEMBLE AND
BAKE THE LASAGNE

PREPARE THE SEAFOOD

Peel shell from prawn
starting at head end,
then tail can be nipped
off easily

1 Peel off the shells from the prawns. Make a shallow cut along the back of each prawn and remove the dark intestinal vein. If the prawns are large, cut them lengthwise in half.

2 If necessary, remove and discard the tough muscle at the side of each scallop. Rinse the scallops with cold water, drain, and pat them dry with paper towels.

Slice across
fillets to cut
into pieces

3 Using the small knife, cut large scallops crosswise in half.

Pieces of fish will
be easy to distribute
evenly in dish

4 Rinse the sole fillets with cold water and pat dry with paper towels. Cut into several pieces. Refrigerate until ready to use.

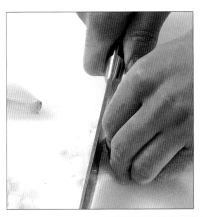

5 Peel the shallots and separate into sections if necessary. Slice horizontally towards the root, leaving the slices attached at the root. Slice vertically, again leaving the root end uncut, then cut across the shallot to make fine dice.

6 Heat the butter in a medium saucepan. Add the chopped shallots and sauté, stirring, until soft but not brown, 1–2 minutes. Add the prawns and scallops, and season with salt and pepper.

Do not overcook
prawns or they
will be tough

Cooking liquid
will enrich sauce

7 Cook over medium heat until the
prawns turn pink and the scallops
become opaque, 2–3 minutes. Add the
white wine and bring just to a boil.

8 Remove the pan
from the heat.
With the slotted spoon,
lift out the prawns and
scallops and reserve them.
Set the cooking liquid aside.

2 MAKE THE SAUCE

1 Peel and quarter the onion. In a
saucepan, combine the onion, bay
leaf, milk, and peppercorns. Bring to a
boil, then cover and keep in a warm
place, 10 minutes. Meanwhile,
peel, deseed, and
chop the tomatoes
(see box, page 64).

ANNE SAYS
*"To save time, you
can use 250 g (8 oz)
drained canned plum
tomatoes."*

Infusing milk
with onion adds
extra flavour

Flavoured milk
makes aromatic
addition to sauce

2 Wipe the mushroom caps with a
damp paper towel and trim the
stalks even with the caps. Set the
mushrooms stalk-side down on the
chopping board and slice them.

3 Add the sliced mushrooms to
the reserved prawn and scallop
cooking liquid and simmer 2 minutes.
Set aside.

Straining removes flavourings

4 Melt the butter in another saucepan over medium heat. Whisk in the flour and cook until foaming, 30–60 seconds.

5 Take the pan from the heat; let cool slightly, then strain in the milk. Whisk to mix. Return to the heat and cook, whisking constantly, until the sauce boils and thickens, 2–3 minutes. Season with salt and pepper and simmer about 2 minutes. Remove from heat.

6 Pour the double cream into the white sauce and then whisk vigorously to mix.

! TAKE CARE !

If the sauce forms lumps at any stage, whisk vigorously off the heat. If whisking is not sufficient, strain the sauce.

7 Add the mushrooms with their cooking liquid to the saucepan, then add the chopped tomatoes. Return the pan to the heat and simmer 2 minutes.

8 Strip the parsley and basil leaves from the stalks and coarsely chop.

Tomatoes and mushrooms give sauce its character

9 Stir the herbs into the sauce with the crushed chillies, salt, and pepper. Set the sauce aside.

HOW TO PEEL, DESEED, AND CHOP TOMATOES

Tomatoes are often peeled and deseeded before chopping so they will cook to form a smooth purée.

1 Bring a small pan of water to a boil. Using a small knife, cut out the cores from the tomatoes. Score an "x" on the base of each tomato. Immerse the tomatoes in the water and boil until the skin starts to split, 8–15 seconds. Using a slotted spoon, transfer them at once to a bowl of cold water to stop cooking.

2 When cold, peel the skin from the tomatoes with a small knife. Cut the tomatoes crosswise in half and squeeze out the seeds.

3 Set each tomato half cut-side down and slice it. Give it a half turn and slice again. Chop the flesh coarsely or finely, as required.

3 ASSEMBLE AND BAKE THE LASAGNE

1 Fill the shallow saucepan with water, bring to a boil, and add the oil and 15 ml (1 tbsp) salt. Add the noodles one by one and simmer until just tender, 3–5 minutes for fresh, 8–10 minutes for dried, or according to package directions.

2 Using the slotted spoon, lift out the lasagne noodles and put them into the colander. Rinse with cold water and drain again thoroughly. When cold, spread out on a clean dish towel to dry. Grate the Gruyère cheese.

3 Heat the oven to 180°C (350°F, Gas 4). Butter the baking dish. Ladle one-quarter of the sauce over the bottom of the prepared dish and arrange half of the prawns and scallops on top.

Dot sauce with prawns and scallops

4 Cover the sauce and prawn and scallop mixture with a layer of lasagne noodles.

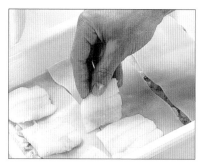

5 Put the fish pieces in one layer on top of the lasagne. Coat the fish with one-third of the remaining sauce and cover with lasagne noodles.

6 Add the rest of the prawns and scallops followed by half of the remaining sauce, then cover with the remaining lasagne noodles. Ladle the remaining sauce evenly over the top. Sprinkle with the grated Gruyère cheese.

Final sprinkling of cheese ensures browned topping

Creamy sauce tops seafood

7 Bake the lasagne in the heated oven until bubbling and golden brown on top, 30–45 minutes.

🍽 TO SERVE
Cut the lasagne into squares and serve hot from the baking dish onto warmed individual plates.

Crispy topping gives crunch and texture

Tomatoes give colour to finished lasagne

SMOKED TROUT AND SPINACH LASAGNE

In this colourful lasagne, smoked trout and prawns are arranged between layers of spinach lasagne noodles.

1 Prepare and cook 500 g (1 lb) raw prawns as directed; omit the scallops.
2 Replace the sole fillets with the same quantity of smoked trout. Cut the trout into large pieces.
3 Make the sauce as directed.
4 Use spinach lasagne noodles in place of plain lasagne noodles.
5 Assemble and bake the lasagne as directed in the main recipe.
6 Serve decorated with salad and herb leaves, if you like.

— GETTING AHEAD —
The seafood and sauce can be prepared, and the lasagne assembled up to 1 day ahead and kept, covered, in the refrigerator. Bake the lasagne just before serving.

STEAMED FISH PLAITS WITH WARM VINAIGRETTE

¶◎¶ SERVES 6 ⌣ WORK TIME 35–40 MINUTES ♨ COOKING TIME 8–10 MINUTES

EQUIPMENT

steamer†

chopping board

saucepan

chef's knife

small knife

fish slice

whisk

paper towels

† large saucepan with lid and rack can also be used

In this recipe, three varieties of fish with different coloured skins are cut into strips, plaited, then steamed over a court bouillon. The plaits are served on individual plates with a warm herb-dotted vinaigrette.

INGREDIENTS

lemon sole fillets†

mackerel fillets†

red snapper fillets†

parsley

onion

shallots

bouquet garni

carrot

olive oil

vegetable oil

Dijon mustard

fresh tarragon

peppercorns

red wine vinegar

cloves

† other suitable fish
any fish with thin, colourful skin such as bass or mullet

metric	SHOPPING LIST	imperial
375 g	red snapper fillets, with their skin	12 oz
375 g	lemon sole fillets, with their skin	12 oz
375 g	mackerel fillets, with their skin	12 oz
	salt and pepper	
	For the court bouillon	
1	carrot	1
1	onion	1
1 litre	water	1¾ pints
1	bouquet garni made with 5–6 parsley stalks, 2–3 sprigs of fresh thyme, and 1 bay leaf	1
6	peppercorns	6
2	whole cloves	2
	For the warm vinaigrette	
2	shallots	2
125 ml	red wine vinegar	4 fl oz
10 ml	Dijon mustard	2 tsp
75 ml	olive oil	2½ fl oz
150 ml	vegetable oil	¼ pint
5–7	sprigs of fresh tarragon or thyme	5–7
7–10	sprigs of fresh parsley or chervil	7–10

ORDER OF WORK

1. **PREPARE COURT BOUILLON AND FISH**

2. **STEAM THE FISH PLAITS**

3. **MAKE THE VINAIGRETTE; FINISH THE DISH**

PREPARE COURT BOUILLON AND FISH

1 Peel and quarter the carrot and onion. Combine the water, bouquet garni, peppercorns, 5 ml (1 tsp) salt, the cloves, carrot, and onion in the bottom of the steamer and bring just to a boil. There should be about 5 cm (2 inches) of court bouillon in the steamer. Simmer 20–30 minutes.

2 Meanwhile, rinse the fish fillets with cold water; pat dry with paper towels. Discard any bones. Trim the fillets so they are roughly the same length.

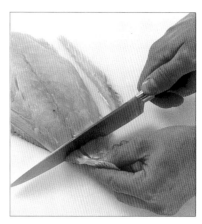

Shimmering snapper contributes to colourful plait

Mackerel skin is beautifully marked

3 Cut each of the fish fillets lengthwise into strips about 2 cm (³/₄ inch) wide, so that there will be 6 strips of each different type of fish to plait.

! TAKE CARE !
Handle fish gently while cutting so strips do not break.

Plait strips loosely so they do not shrink and break during cooking

Plaits do not have to be even

4 Arrange a strip of snapper, sole, and mackerel next to each other, skin-side up. Plait the strips together, lifting them carefully over each other and gathering the ends together. Continue making plaits with the remaining strips of fish.

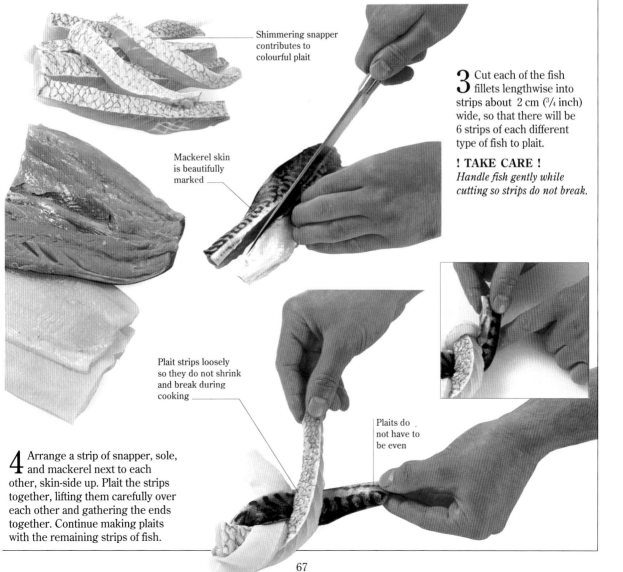

HOW TO CHOP HERBS

Parsley, tarragon, thyme, chives, rosemary, dill, and basil are herbs that are usually chopped before being added to other ingredients. Do not chop delicate herbs like basil too finely because their leaves bruise easily.

Pull off herb leaves gently to ensure they retain maximum freshness

1 Strip the leaves or sprigs from the stalks. Pile the leaves or sprigs on a chopping board.

2 Cut the leaves or sprigs into small pieces, holding the herbs together in a bunch with one hand while chopping with a chef's knife. Holding the tip of the knife blade against the chopping board with your fingertips, and rocking the blade back and forth, chop until the herbs are coarse or fine, as you wish.

2 STEAM THE FISH PLAITS

1 Using the fish slice, transfer the plaits to the steamer rack. Sprinkle them with salt and pepper.

ANNE SAYS
"You may have to steam the fish plaits in 2 batches."

Season plaits to taste

Leave space between plaits in steamer

2 Set the rack over the simmering court bouillon; there should still be 5 cm (2 inches) of liquid.

! TAKE CARE !
If too much liquid evaporates from the steamer, add more water.

3 Cover the steamer and steam the fish until it just flakes easily when tested with a fork, 8–10 minutes. Meanwhile, make the vinaigrette.

3 MAKE THE VINAIGRETTE; FINISH THE DISH

1 Peel each shallot and slice
  horizontally towards the root,
leaving the slices attached at the root.
Slice vertically, then cut across the
shallot to make fine dice. Strip the
herb leaves from the stalks, reserving
4 sprigs of each for garnish. Finely
chop the leaves (see box, page 68).

2 In the saucepan, whisk together
  the vinegar, mustard, and shallots.
Add the olive oil, then the vegetable oil
in a steady stream, whisking constantly
so the vinaigrette emulsifies and
thickens slightly. Heat gently until
warm, whisking constantly. Remove
from the heat and whisk in the herbs
and salt and pepper to taste.

🍴 TO SERVE
Spoon the vinaigrette onto 6 warmed
individual plates. Transfer the plaits to
the plates. Garnish with the reserved
parsley and tarragon
sprigs, and serve
at once.

Fish plaits make a
spectacular presentation

VARIATION

PANACHE OF STEAMED FISH WITH WARM SHERRY VINAIGRETTE

*A "panaché", or selection, of
fish features here with a warm
sherry vinaigrette as
accompaniment. French beans
are a good complement.*

1 Make the court bouillon as directed.
2 Rinse the fish fillets and pat dry. Cut
the fish into even diamond shapes.
3 Steam the fish pieces as for the
braids, allowing 5–7 minutes,
depending on their thickness. If the
steamer is crowded, cook the fish
pieces in 2 batches.
4 Meanwhile, prepare the warm
vinaigrette as directed in the main
recipe, substituting sherry vinegar
for the red wine vinegar and walnut
oil for the olive oil. Omit the herbs.
5 Arrange the fish on warmed
individual plates, skin-side up.
Spoon a little of the warm sherry
vinaigrette over the fish and serve
the remainder separately.

——— GETTING AHEAD ———
The vinaigrette can be made up to
1 day ahead. The court bouillon can be
made and the fish plaited up to 1 hour
ahead. Just before serving, warm the
vinaigrette and add the herbs while the
fish is steaming.

MONKFISH AMERICAINE

EQUIPMENT

saucepans

kitchen scissors

bowl

kitchen string

vegetable peeler

filleting knife

sauté pan†

chef's knife

small ladle

sieve

paper towels

wooden spoon

whisk

palette knife

chopping board

† large frying pan can also be used

Known as the poor man's lobster for its sweetness and "meaty" texture, monkfish has grown increasingly popular in recent years. Here, it is served with a tomato, garlic, and Cognac sauce.

metric	SHOPPING LIST	imperial
1.4 kg	piece of monkfish, on the bone	3 lb
2	medium onions	2
125 ml	white wine or juice of ½ lemon	4 fl oz
5 ml	peppercorns	1 tsp
3–5	sprigs of parsley	3–5
500 ml	water	16 fl oz
30 g	plain flour	1 oz
	salt and pepper	
30 ml	olive oil	2 tbsp
125 g	butter	4 oz
	rice pilaf (see box, page 74) for serving (optional)	
	For the américaine sauce	
1	carrot	1
2	garlic cloves	2
750 g	tomatoes	1½ lb
3–4	sprigs of fresh tarragon	3–4
1	bouquet garni (see box, page 72)	1
150 ml	white wine	¼ pint
45 ml	Cognac	3 tbsp
1	pinch of cayenne pepper (optional)	1
15 ml	tomato purée	1 tbsp
60 ml	double cream	4 tbsp
1	pinch of sugar (optional)	1

INGREDIENTS

monkfish†

carrot

white wine   parsley sprigs

onions

double cream

tomatoes

olive oil

plain flour

peppercorns

garlic cloves

tomato purée

Cognac

bouquet garni

butter

fresh tarragon

† other suitable fish
huss

ORDER OF WORK

1   **PREPARE THE MONKFISH**

2   **MAKE THE STOCK; PREPARE SAUCE INGREDIENTS**

3   **COOK THE FISH; MAKE THE SAUCE**

1 PREPARE THE MONKFISH

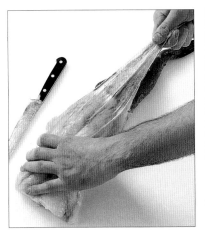

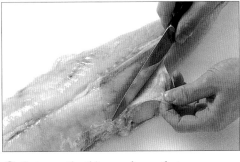

ANNE SAYS
"The spine in monkfish has no lateral bones, so once the skin and covering thin white membrane have been removed, the fish can be filleted easily, to yield 2 thick boneless pieces of meat."

2 Cut away the thin membrane that covers the fish, cutting close to the flesh with the filleting knife, and pulling the membrane away from the fish with your fingers.

1 If necessary, skin the monkfish: using the filleting knife, cut and release the black skin, then pull it off.

Keep knife blade close to backbone while cutting away whole fillet

3 Cut along one side of the central backbone to remove 1 monkfish fillet. Repeat the process on the other side of the bone to remove the second fillet. Rinse the monkfish fillets with cold water and pat them dry with paper towels.

Ease fillet away from bone with fingertips as you cut

Fillets are easy to remove from central backbone

Cut slices of uniform thickness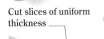

5 Cut each fillet into 1 cm (1/2 inch) slices. Slightly flatten each slice with the side of the chef's knife.

4 With the chef's knife, cut the bone in pieces and reserve the pieces for the fish stock.

MAKE THE STOCK; PREPARE SAUCE INGREDIENTS

1 Peel and chop the onions. Put half of the chopped onions in a large saucepan and add the monkfish bones, wine, peppercorns, parsley, and water.

2 Bring the mixture slowly to a boil, then simmer, uncovered, 20 minutes. Strain the fish stock into the bowl and let cool. You should have about 500 ml (16 fl oz) of stock.

HOW TO MAKE A BOUQUET GARNI

This package of aromatic flavouring herbs is designed to be easily lifted from the pan and discarded at the end of cooking. To make a bouquet garni, hold together 2–3 sprigs of fresh thyme, 1 bay leaf, and 5–6 parsley stalks. Wind a piece of string around the herb stalks and tie them together securely, leaving a length of string to tie the bouquet garni to the pan handle.

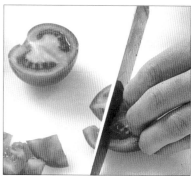

3 While the stock is cooling, peel and trim the carrot. Cut it lengthwise into quarters, then across into 1 cm (½ inch) pieces. Set the flat side of the chef's knife on top of each garlic clove and strike it with your fist. Discard the skin and finely chop the garlic.

4 Remove the cores from the tomatoes, then cut each tomato in half. Coarsely chop the halves.

ANNE SAYS
"You will not need to peel and deseed the tomatoes because the sauce will be sieved."

Herbs infuse ingredients with fresh aroma

Wind string around herb stalks

5 Strip the tarragon leaves from the stalks and pile them on the chopping board. Coarsely chop the leaves and reserve for garnish. Set aside the stalks for the sauce.

Sharp chef's knife makes chopping herbs easy

Tear leaves gently from stalks to avoid bruising

3 COOK THE FISH; MAKE THE SAUCE

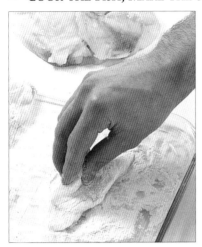

1 Put the flour on a plate and season with salt and pepper. Lightly coat the monkfish slices with the seasoned flour, patting with your hands so the slices are evenly coated.

2 Heat the oil and one-quarter of the butter in the sauté pan, add half of the fish slices and sauté, turning once, until brown on both sides, 2–3 minutes. Transfer the slices to a plate with the palette knife. Sauté the remaining monkfish slices and transfer to the plate.

3 Add the carrot, garlic, and the remaining onion to the sauté pan and cook, stirring to mix in the browned flour from the bottom of the pan, until soft but not brown, 3–5 minutes.

4 Add the tomatoes, white wine, Cognac, tarragon stalks, salt and pepper, and a pinch of cayenne pepper, if you like. Tie the bouquet garni to the pan handle. Pour in the stock. Bring to a boil and simmer until slightly thickened, 15–20 minutes.

Bouquet garni tied to handle of pan will be easy to remove before sauce is sieved

5 Sieve the sauce into a large saucepan, pressing with the ladle to extract all the liquid from the ingredients. Boil until thickened and reduced, 5–10 minutes.

6 Whisk in the double cream and tomato purée until the sauce is an even colour. Taste the sauce for seasoning, adding a pinch of sugar if it is too acidic.

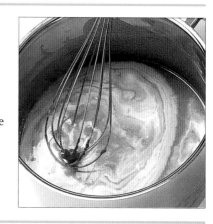

RICE PILAF

When making pilaf, the rice is first quickly fried in vegetable oil to help keep the grains separate as the rice simmers. It is then cooked in a measured amount of water so the liquid is all absorbed during cooking, leaving the rice light, tender, and flaky.

1 Peel and chop the onion. Heat the oil in a heavy-based saucepan, add the onion, and cook, stirring, until soft but not brown, 1–2 minutes.

2 Add the rice and cook, stirring, until the oil is absorbed and the rice looks translucent, 2–3 minutes.

Stir rice in oil to keep grains separate

🍽 SERVES 4–6

🥣 WORK TIME 5–10 MINUTES

🍲 COOKING TIME 20 MINUTES

SHOPPING LIST

1	medium onion	1
30 ml	vegetable oil	2 tbsp
300 g	long-grain rice	10 oz
750 ml	water	1¼ pints
	salt and pepper	

3 Pour the water into the saucepan, season the rice with salt and pepper, and bring to a boil.

4 Cover the pan, reduce the heat, and simmer until all the liquid is absorbed and the rice is tender, about 20 minutes. Let stand, still covered, 10 minutes, then stir with a fork.

7 Add the monkfish slices to the sauce and simmer until just tender, 5–10 minutes.

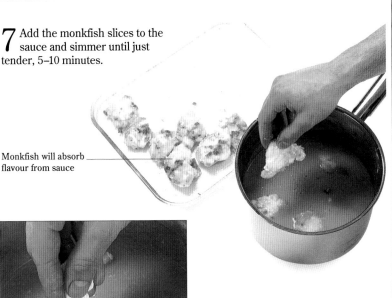

Monkfish will absorb flavour from sauce

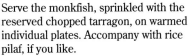

8 Take the saucepan from the heat and add the remaining butter, in small pieces, shaking the saucepan so the butter melts and is mixed into the sauce.

🍴 **TO SERVE**
Serve the monkfish, sprinkled with the reserved chopped tarragon, on warmed individual plates. Accompany with rice pilaf, if you like.

Monkfish slices are just tender to the bite

VARIATION
SALT COD AMERICAINE

1 Soak 750 g (1½ lb) salt cod in cold water 1–2 days, changing the water several times. Drain and put in a large pan of cold water, cover, and bring just to a boil. Simmer until barely tender, 8–10 minutes. Drain and let cool slightly. Flake the cod with a fork, discarding any skin and bones.
2 Make the américaine sauce, using water if you have no fish bones for stock, and omitting the tarragon. Peel and deseed the tomatoes before chopping: cut out the cores and score an "x" on the base of each. Immerse in boiling water until the skin starts to split, 8–15 seconds. Transfer at once to cold water. When cold, peel off the skin. Cut crosswise in half and squeeze out the seeds. Finish the sauce as directed but do not sieve it. Discard the bouquet garni.
3 While the sauce is simmering, make rice pilaf (see box, page 74).
4 Add the flaked salt cod to the sauce and cook until tender, 5–10 minutes.
5 Pack the hot rice pilaf into each of 6 buttered ramekins (225 ml/7 fl oz). Let stand 2 minutes, then unmould onto warmed individual plates. Spoon the salt cod and sauce beside the rice. Decorate with fresh dill sprigs.

GETTING AHEAD
The monkfish and sauce can be cooked up to 1 day ahead and kept, covered, in the refrigerator. Reheat on top of the stove, taking care not to overcook the fish or it will become tough.

TURBANS OF SOLE WITH WILD MUSHROOM MOUSSE

 SERVES 4 WORK TIME 20–25 MINUTES* BAKING TIME 35–45 MINUTES

EQUIPMENT

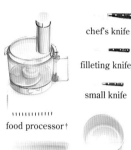

chef's knife

filleting knife

small knife

food processor†

750 ml
(1¼ pint)
soufflé dish

baking dishes

bowls

pastry brush

frying pans

piping bag with
large nozzle‡   chopping board

palette knife

wooden
cocktail sticks   wooden spoon

whisk

paper
towels
aluminium foil

rubber spatula
† blender can also be used
‡ star or plain nozzle can be used

INGREDIENTS

lemon sole fillets†

fresh shiitake   double cream
mushrooms

butter

dry white   Madeira
wine

egg

egg yolk

fresh coriander

† other suitable fish
plaice, turbot

Sole fillets are shaped into rings, turban-fashion, and filled with a shiitake mushroom mousse. Although most shiitake mushrooms are now cultivated rather than wild, they still retain their wild, "earthy" flavour.

GETTING AHEAD

The mousse can be made up to 1 day ahead and kept refrigerated. Bake the turbans just before serving.

* plus 1 hour chilling time

metric	SHOPPING LIST	imperial
6	skinless lemon sole fillets, total weight about 500 g (1 lb)	6
125 ml	dry white wine	4 fl oz
3–5	sprigs of fresh coriander, more for garnish	3–5
125 g	butter, chilled	4 oz
	For the wild mushroom mousse	
150 g	fresh, or 30 g (1 oz) dried, shiitake mushrooms	5 oz
2–3	sprigs of fresh coriander	2–3
30 g	butter, more for dishes and foil	1 oz
	salt and pepper	
1	egg	1
1	egg yolk	1
15 ml	Madeira	1 tbsp
125 ml	double cream	4 fl oz

ORDER OF WORK

1 MAKE THE WILD MUSHROOM MOUSSE

2 PREPARE AND BAKE THE SOLE TURBANS

3 MAKE THE CORIANDER SAUCE

1 MAKE THE WILD MUSHROOM MOUSSE

1 Wipe fresh shiitake mushrooms with damp paper towels and trim the stalks, using the small knife. Cut the mushrooms into medium slices. Strip the leaves from the coriander stalks and roughly chop.

ANNE SAYS
"If using dried shiitake mushrooms, soak them in a bowl of warm water until they are plump, about 30 minutes. Drain them and then continue as for fresh mushrooms."

Curl fingers to hold mushroom cap securely when slicing

Set mushrooms stalk-side down to slice

2 Heat the butter in a medium frying pan. Add the mushrooms with salt and pepper. Cook, stirring constantly, until the liquid has all evaporated, 3–5 minutes. Remove from the heat and let the mixture cool slightly.

Transfer mixture to bowl for chilling

3 Put the mushrooms in the food processor and purée them. With the blade turning, add the whole egg and the egg yolk. Purée until smooth. Add the Madeira and coriander leaves, and purée just until combined.

4 Mix in salt and pepper, then transfer the puréed mushroom mixture to a bowl. Cover and chill about 1 hour. Fold the cream into the mushroom mixture.

Scrape all mixture from bowl with rubber spatula

5 Heat the oven to 190°C (375°F, Gas 5). Brush the inside of the soufflé dish with melted butter.

Mousse mixture will not stick to buttered dish

6 Using the rubber spatula, transfer the chilled mousse mixture from the bowl to the prepared soufflé dish.

Pour hot water carefully around soufflé dish so that liquid does not splash into mousse

Be sure hot water comes well up side of dish so heat is diffused

7 Set the soufflé dish in a baking dish. Pour sufficient hot water into the baking dish to come halfway up the side of the soufflé dish.

8 Transfer the baking dish to the heated oven and bake until just set when lightly pressed, 20–25 minutes. Remove the soufflé dish from the water; let the mousse cool while preparing the sole turbans. Reduce oven temperature to 180°C (350°F, Gas 4).

2 PREPARE AND BAKE THE SOLE TURBANS

1 Rinse the sole fillets with cold water. Transfer them to paper towels and carefully pat the fillets dry.

2 With the filleting knife, cut each of the sole fillets lengthwise in half.

Wooden cocktail sticks hold rings of sole in place

Halved sole fillets make perfect turban shapes

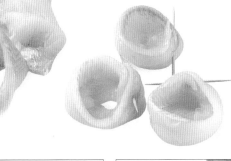

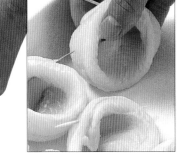

3 Shape each fillet half into a 7.5 cm (3 inch) ring, skinned-side in, with the tail end around the outside. Secure with cocktail sticks. Brush a shallow baking dish with some melted butter, then arrange the sole in the dish.

4 Fold the top of the piping bag, fitted with the large star nozzle, over your hand to form a collar. Spoon in the wild mushroom mousse.

5 Twist the top of the bag, then pipe the mousse in a swirl into the centre of each sole ring so that each of the rings is completely filled.

6 Carefully pour the white wine around the sole turbans in the baking dish.

Stuffed turbans cooked in white wine will keep moist in oven

7 Butter a piece of foil and use to cover the sole turbans in the baking dish.

Cooking liquid is essential to sauce

8 Bake in the heated oven until the fish is white and opaque, and the mousse is firm to the touch, 15–20 minutes.

9 Transfer the sole turbans to a warmed serving plate and reserve the cooking liquid. Remove cocktail sticks. Keep the turbans warm while making the sauce.

MAKE THE CORIANDER SAUCE

1 Strip the leaves from the coriander stalks, then pile the leaves on the chopping board. With the chef's knife, finely chop the leaves.

2 Cut the chilled butter into small even-sized pieces, using the small knife.

3 Pour the cooking liquid from the dish into a small frying pan. Boil until reduced to about 30 ml (2 tbsp).

Add butter pieces gradually

4 Take from the heat and add the butter, a little at a time, whisking constantly and moving the pan on and off the heat. The sauce should thicken to a creamy consistency.

Coriander sauce
adds colour and richness
to stuffed sole turbans

5 Whisk in the chopped coriander. Taste the sauce for seasoning.

🍴 TO SERVE
Pour the coriander sauce over and around the sole turbans. Garnish each turban with a fresh coriander leaf.

VARIATION
TURBANS OF PLAICE WITH SPINACH MOUSSE

Green spinach mousse makes a pretty filling for turbans of plaice, served here with a tomato-flavoured butter sauce.

1 Discard the stalks from 750 g (1½ lb) fresh spinach; wash the leaves thoroughly. Bring a large pan of water to a boil, add salt, then the spinach, and blanch 1 minute. Drain in a colander, rinse with cold water, and squeeze to remove all water.
2 Make the mousse as directed, replacing the shiitake mushrooms with spinach and omitting the Madeira. Add a pinch of ground coriander with the salt and pepper.
3 Replace the sole with 6 plaice fillets, weighing about 500 g (1 lb), and prepare and shape into rings as directed.
4 Fill the plaice rings with the cooked spinach mousse and bake as directed.
5 Make the sauce, omitting the fresh coriander. Whisk in 15 ml (1 tbsp) tomato purée after all the butter has been added.
6 Serve the plaice turbans on warmed individual plates with the butter sauce spooned around them. Sautéed sliced new potatoes are an ideal accompaniment.

TWO-COLOUR FISH TERRINE WITH CITRUS-GINGER SAUCE

🍽 SERVES 8　🥄 WORK TIME 30–35 MINUTES　🍲 BAKING TIME 1¼–1½ HOURS

EQUIPMENT

30 x 8.5 x 7.5 cm
(12 x 3½ x 3 inch)
terrine mould with lid

slotted spoon　　small knife†

metal skewer

rubber spatula

sieve　　　saucepans

whisk

vegetable peeler

lemon
squeezer

wooden spoon

chef's knife

filleting knife

food processor　pastry brush

roasting tin　　bowls

paper towels

†tweezers can also be used

In this fish terrine, a duo of sole fillets and a smooth salmon mousseline create a contrast of colour and flavour. A simple butter sauce is served with the terrine, which makes a good main-course luncheon dish when accompanied by lightly cooked asparagus.

GETTING AHEAD

The terrine can be baked 1 day ahead and kept, covered, in the refrigerator. Before serving, reheat it in a bain-marie on top of the stove, allowing 10–15 minutes, with the water at a simmer. Make the sauce just before serving.

metric	SHOPPING LIST	imperial
750 g	fresh salmon fillet	1½ lb
3	egg whites	3
	salt and pepper	
375 ml	double cream	12 fl oz
4	sole fillets	4
	butter for terrine mould	
2	slices smoked salmon, total weight about 90 g (3 oz)	2
	For the citrus-ginger sauce	
3–5	sprigs of parsley	3–5
2.5 cm	piece of fresh root ginger	1 inch
1	lemon	1
1	lime	1
45 ml	double cream	3 tbsp
175 g	unsalted butter, chilled	6 oz

INGREDIENTS

fresh salmon fillet†

sole fillets　　smoked salmon

fresh root ginger

lemon

lime　　　　parsley sprigs

unsalted
butter

egg whites　double cream

†other suitable fish
plaice, salmon trout

ORDER OF WORK

1　PREPARE THE SALMON MOUSSELINE

2　ASSEMBLE AND BAKE THE TERRINE

3　MAKE THE CITRUS-GINGER SAUCE

PREPARE THE SALMON MOUSSELINE

1 Run the blade of the small knife over the salmon fillet to find any bones. Pinch the bones between your thumb and the small knife blade and pull to remove them.

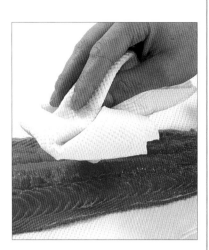

2 If necessary, skin the salmon fillet. Rinse the salmon with cold water and pat dry, then cut into pieces.

ANNE SAYS
"To skin the fillet, set skin-side down and, holding the tail, cut through to the skin at the tail end. Cut the flesh from the skin."

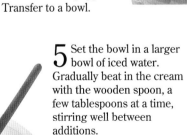

After adding egg white, mousseline mixture is smooth and quite stiff

3 Put the salmon pieces in the food processor. Work the fish until smooth, using the pulse button and scraping down the side with the rubber spatula.

! TAKE CARE !
Do not overwork the fish or it will be tough when cooked.

4 Gradually add the egg whites. Using the pulse button, work the mixture until smooth, 1–2 minutes, scraping down the side with the rubber spatula. Mix in salt and pepper. Transfer to a bowl.

Pour cream into cool mixture a little at a time

5 Set the bowl in a larger bowl of iced water. Gradually beat in the cream with the wooden spoon, a few tablespoons at a time, stirring well between additions.

ANNE SAYS
"It is best to work in the cream by hand because the mixture could separate if overworked in the food processor."

6 Bring a small saucepan of water to a boil. Drop in a little mousseline mixture and simmer until it is firm, 2–3 minutes; it will become lighter in colour. Taste it and add salt and pepper to the rest of the mousseline mixture, if needed. Cover the bowl and chill.

2 ASSEMBLE AND BAKE THE TERRINE

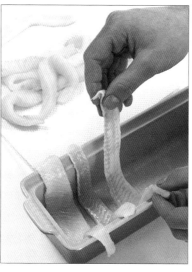

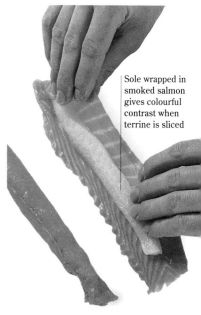

Sole wrapped in smoked salmon gives colourful contrast when terrine is sliced

1 Heat the oven to 180°C (350°F, Gas 4). If necessary, skin the sole fillets. Rinse the fillets and pat them dry, then cut each fillet lengthwise in half. Brush the inside of the terrine mould and lid with melted butter.

2 Line the terrine mould with 6 of the sole fillet pieces, arranging them crosswise and skinned side inwards.

ANNE SAYS
"Leave gaps between the sole fillet pieces so that the pink salmon mousseline can show through."

3 Wrap each remaining sole fillet lengthwise in a slice of smoked salmon, tucking in the ends neatly.

4 Put one-third of the salmon mousseline into the terrine and spread it evenly with the spatula.

Spread mousseline carefully in mould to avoid air pockets

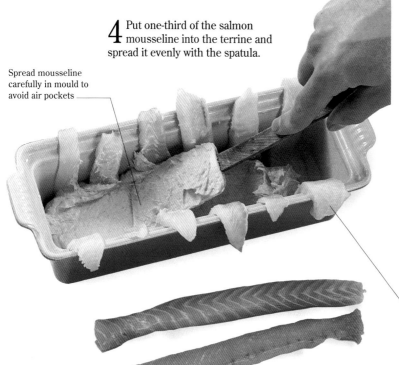

5 Arrange 1 of the smoked salmon and sole fillet cylinders lengthwise on top of the mousseline. Spread another third of the salmon mousseline in the terrine. Top with the second wrapped sole fillet.

Overhanging sole fillets will be wrapped over top when terrine is full

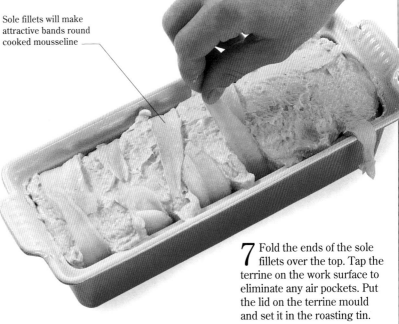

Sole fillets will make attractive bands round cooked mousseline

6 Cover with the remaining mousseline. Using the rubber spatula, smooth the top and press the filling well into the mould.

7 Fold the ends of the sole fillets over the top. Tap the terrine on the work surface to eliminate any air pockets. Put the lid on the terrine mould and set it in the roasting tin.

8 Add hot water to the tin to come just over halfway up the terrine mould. Bring this bain-marie to a boil on top of the stove, then transfer the terrine in the tin to the heated oven.

Water should come more than halfway up sides of mould

Water bath ensures terrine cooks evenly

9 Bake until the skewer inserted in the terrine 30 seconds is hot to the touch when withdrawn, 1¼–1½ hours. Take the terrine from the oven and let stand 5–10 minutes while you make the sauce.

ANNE SAYS
"You can insert the skewer into the terrine through the hole in the lid of the mould."

3 MAKE THE CITRUS-GINGER SAUCE

Gently tear leaves from stalks with fingers

Leftover parsley stalks are good for flavouring stock and making bouquet garni

1
Strip the parsley leaves from the stalks and pile them on the chopping board. With the chef's knife, finely chop the leaves. Peel and finely chop the ginger (see box, below left).

2
Using the vegetable peeler, pare the zest from the lemon. Cut the zest into fine strips. Squeeze the juice from the lemon and reserve it. Squeeze the juice from the lime and reserve.

HOW TO PEEL AND CHOP FRESH ROOT GINGER

It is important to chop root ginger very finely, so the flavour spreads evenly throughout the dish.

1
With a small knife, peel the skin from the root ginger. Using a chef's knife, slice the ginger, cutting across the fibrous grain; place the knife flat on each slice and crush with your hand.

2
Chop the slices of root ginger as finely as possible.

Blanching lemon zest removes any bitterness

3
Bring a small saucepan of water to a boil, add the strips of lemon zest, and simmer 2 minutes. Drain in the sieve and set aside.

4
In a small, heavy-based saucepan, boil the ginger and lemon juice until reduced to 15 ml (1 tbsp), about 1 minute. Add the cream and boil until reduced to 30 ml (2 tbsp), about 2 minutes. Cut the butter into pieces.

5
Take the pan from the heat and add the butter, a few pieces at a time, whisking constantly and moving the pan on and off the heat. The butter should thicken the sauce to a creamy consistency without melting to oil.

Lime juice gives sauce extra citrus tang

6 Add the parsley, lemon zest, and lime juice to the sauce. Whisk into the sauce until mixed.

7 Holding the lid firmly on the mould, tip it sideways over the saucepan to drain 15–30 ml (1–2 tbsp) liquid into the sauce. Whisk to mix. Discard the remaining liquid from the terrine. Season the sauce to taste.

🍽 **TO SERVE**

Turn out the terrine. Cut it into 2 cm (³/₄ inch) slices and serve on pools of sauce on warmed individual plates, alternating sole-banded mousseline slices with unbanded slices.

Pink slices of salmon mousseline are studded with sole circled by smoked salmon

Asparagus decorated with shreds of lemon zest is complementary accompaniment

VARIATION

INDIVIDUAL FISH TERRINES

Here, ramekins serve as moulds for fish terrines. Thin slices of salmon line the moulds, with a whiting or sole mousseline filling. The recipe serves 4 people.

1 Butter 4 ramekins (225 ml/7 fl oz capacity). Prepare a 375 g (12 oz) piece of fresh salmon fillet as directed. Holding the salmon steady and working towards the tail, use a filleting knife to cut diagonal slices about 3 mm (¹/₈ inch) thick. Cut the slices in half. Line the ramekins with the slices of salmon, allowing excess to overhang.
2 Prepare the mousseline as directed, using 500 g (1 lb) whiting or sole fillets in place of the salmon. Omit the smoked salmon and additional fish.
3 Spoon the mousseline into the prepared ramekins, smoothing the tops and pressing the filling well into the moulds. Fold the salmon edges over the filling, and arrange any remaining salmon slices on top.
4 Cover each with a small round of buttered foil and cook in a bain-marie as directed, allowing 30–40 minutes.
5 Make the citrus-ginger sauce as directed, but reserve the lemon zest for garnish.
6 Turn out the terrines onto warmed individual plates and spoon the sauce around them. Garnish each terrine with lemon zest; decorate with peeled lime segments and parsley sprigs, if you like.

BOUILLABAISSE

🍽 SERVES 8–10 🥣 WORK TIME 50–55 MINUTES* 🍲 COOKING TIME 50–60 MINUTES

EQUIPMENT

whisk

small knife

chef's knife

vegetable peeler

bowls

large flameproof casserole

sieve

slotted spoon

ladle

wooden spoon

colander

saucepans

kitchen string

paper towels

aluminium foil

chopping board

Purists maintain that a true bouillabaisse cannot be made away from the Mediterranean. However, you can create an excellent version based on local fish – possible white fish include cod, haddock, hake, red gurnard, red snapper, and whiting, while among the oily fish are eel, mackerel, and herring.

*plus 1–2 hours marinating time

INGREDIENTS

mixed white fish

tomatoes

leeks

mixed oily fish

garlic cloves

olive oil

fennel bulb

bouquet garni

onions

Pernod

parsley

orange

tomato purée

celery

saffron threads

ANNE SAYS
"Ask your fishmonger to trim and scale the fish."

ORDER OF WORK

1 PREPARE THE FISH, MARINADE, AND STOCK

2 PREPARE THE BROTH

3 FINISH THE BOUILLABAISSE

metric	SHOPPING LIST	imperial
1.4 kg	mixed white fish, cleaned, on bone, with heads	3 lb
1 kg	mixed oily fish, cleaned, scaled, on bone	2 lb
2	large pinches of saffron threads	2
5–6	garlic cloves	5–6
125 ml	olive oil	4 fl oz
2	medium onions	2
2	medium leeks	2
2	celery sticks	2
1	fennel bulb or 5 ml (1 tsp) dried fennel seed	1
500 g	tomatoes	1 lb
1	orange	1
10–12	sprigs of parsley	10–12
1	bouquet garni made with 5–6 parsley stalks, 2–3 sprigs of fresh thyme, and 1 bay leaf	1
15 ml	tomato purée	1 tbsp
15 ml	Pernod or other aniseed-flavoured liqueur	1 tbsp
	croûtes (see box, page 89) and Quick Chilli Mayonnaise (see box, page 92) for serving (optional)	

PREPARE THE FISH, MARINADE, AND STOCK

Saffron gives marinade striking yellow colour

1 Rinse the fish inside and out, drain, and pat dry with paper towels. Keeping the white and oily fish separate, cut all the fish across into 5 cm (2 inch) chunks. Reserve the heads and tails for the stock.

ANNE SAYS
"Rinse the fish heads thoroughly to remove any blood which would make the stock bitter."

2 Make the marinade: put 1 large pinch of saffron threads in a small bowl and add 30 ml (2 tbsp) boiling water. Let the saffron soak 10 minutes. Meanwhile, peel and finely chop 2 garlic cloves (see box, page 91). Combine the saffron and its liquid, the finely chopped garlic, and 45 ml (3 tbsp) olive oil in a bowl. Stir to mix.

3 Put the white fish chunks in one large non-metallic bowl and the oily fish in another non-metallic bowl. Add half of the marinade to each bowl.

HOW TO MAKE CROUTES

Croûtes – larger versions of the well-known croûtons – are the classic accompaniment to a Provençal bouillabaisse. Here, they are brushed lightly with olive oil and toasted until crisp and browned.

Toast croûtes until dry and lightly browned

1 Heat the oven to 180°C (350°F, Gas 4). Put 2 cm (¾ inch) slices of French bread on a baking sheet.

2 Brush the slices lightly with olive oil. Turn them over and brush the other side of each slice.

3 Bake in the heated oven until light brown, 10–12 minutes.

4 Toss the fish to coat thoroughly. Cover and marinate 1–2 hours in the refrigerator.

Stir fish to coat in marinade and ensure flavours are thoroughly absorbed

Keep oily fish separate from white fish because they will cook at different speeds

5 Meanwhile, make the fish stock: put the heads and tails in a large saucepan, add water barely to cover and bring to a boil. Simmer 20 minutes.

6 Pour the fish stock through the sieve into a bowl and set aside.

PREPARE THE BROTH

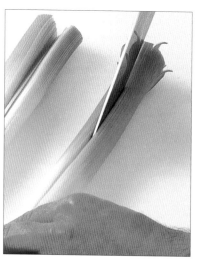

Use tender pale green part of leek tops as well as white portion

1 Peel the onions, leaving a little of the root attached, and cut them in half through the root and stalk. Lay each onion half flat on the chopping board and cut across into thin slices.

2 Trim the leeks, discarding the roots and the tough green tops. Slit them lengthwise and wash thoroughly under running water.

3 Cut the leeks crosswise into thin slices using the chef's knife.

4 With the vegetable peeler, remove the tough strings from each of the celery sticks.

5 Trim the ends from the celery sticks and cut crosswise into thin slices.

Flavour of thinly sliced celery will spread evenly through dish

After strings are removed, celery is easy to slice

6 Trim the base and the feathery green fronds from the fennel bulb.

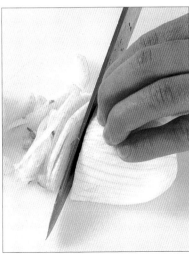

7 Cut the bulb lengthwise in half, then cut each half into thin slices.

HOW TO PEEL AND CHOP GARLIC

The strength of garlic varies with its age and dryness. Use more when it is very fresh.

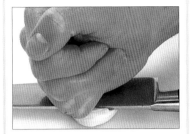

1 To separate the garlic cloves, crush the bulb with the heel of your hand. Alternatively, pull a clove from the bulb with your fingers. To peel the clove, lightly crush it with the flat of the chef's knife to loosen the skin.

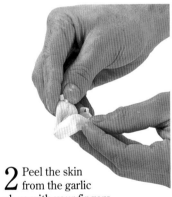

2 Peel the skin from the garlic clove with your fingers.

3 To crush the clove, set the flat side of the knife on top and strike firmly with your fist. Finely chop the garlic with the knife, moving the blade back and forth.

8 Cut the cores from the tomatoes and score an "x" on the base of each with the tip of a knife. Immerse in a pan of boiling water until the skin starts to split, 8–15 seconds depending on their ripeness. Using the slotted spoon, transfer them at once to a bowl of cold water. When cold, peel off the skin. Cut the tomatoes crosswise in half and squeeze out the seeds; coarsely chop each half.

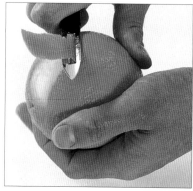

The deeper the colour of the tomato, the more flavour it will have

9 Peel a wide strip of zest from the orange with the vegetable peeler. Peel and coarsely chop the remaining garlic cloves.

QUICK CHILLI MAYONNAISE

For this quick version of the classic "rouille" or rust-red mayonnaise, bottled mayonnaise and tomato purée are added to chilli and garlic.

 SERVES 8–10

 WORK TIME 10 MINUTES

SHOPPING LIST		
1	small fresh red chilli	1
4	garlic cloves, or to taste	4
	salt and pepper	
175 ml	bottled mayonnaise	6 fl oz
5 ml	tomato purée	1 tsp
	cayenne pepper (optional)	

1 Cut the chilli lengthwise in half; discard the core. Scrape out the seeds and cut away the fleshy white ribs from each half. Lightly crush the garlic cloves with the flat of a knife, then peel off the skin.

! TAKE CARE !
Wear rubber gloves to prepare chilli or it may burn your skin.

2 Put the chilli halves in a food processor with the garlic, salt, and pepper, and finely chop.

Tomato purée gives mayonnaise appealing orange tinge

3 Add the bottled mayonnaise and tomato purée; work until smooth. Taste for seasoning and add cayenne pepper, if you like. Chill until serving.

10 Strip the parsley leaves from the stalks and pile them on the chopping board.

11 Coarsely chop the parsley leaves. Soak the remaining pinch of saffron threads in 45–60 ml (3–4 tbsp) boiling water, 10 minutes.

12 Heat the remaining oil in the casserole. Add the onions, leeks, celery, and fennel (or fennel seed). Cook, stirring, 5–7 minutes.

13 Add the tomatoes, orange zest, garlic, and chopped parsley to the casserole.

14 Tie the bouquet garni to the handle of the casserole. Pour in the fish stock. Add the saffron with its liquid and season with salt and pepper. Bring to a boil.

Variety of vegetables will make rich combination of flavours

Fresh taste of parsley is essential accent to dish

15 Simmer the broth until it has thickened and the flavour is mellow, 30–40 minutes, stirring occasionally.

FINISH THE BOUILLABAISSE

1 Bring the broth back to a boil. Add the oily fish and boil fiercely, 7 minutes. Shake the casserole from time to time to prevent the mixture from sticking; do not stir or the fish will disintegrate.

ANNE SAYS
"*It is important to keep the liquid boiling rapidly so that the oil emulsifies with the broth and does not float on the surface.*"

Oily fish go into bouillabaisse first because they take longer to cook

Fish will absorb flavour of broth while cooking

2 Add the white fish pieces to the casserole. Set the pieces of the most delicate types of fish on top of the bouillabaisse.

4 With the slotted spoon, transfer the fish to a hot serving platter, arranging them so the different kinds are separated. Cover with foil to keep warm.

3 Continue boiling until the fish just flakes easily with a fork, 5–8 minutes. If necessary, add more water during cooking so the fish remains covered.

Transfer fish carefully or it may fall apart

5 Discard the bouquet garni and orange zest from the broth and whisk in the tomato purée and Pernod. Taste the broth for seasoning.

🍽 **TO SERVE**

Ladle the broth into a soup tureen and serve at once, with the fish. Serve croûtes and chilli mayonnaise on the side, if you like.

Fish is served separately from broth; guests can help themselves to each

V A R I A T I O N
CREOLE BOUILLABAISSE

Shellfish, such as oysters and scampi, added to the selection of white and oily fish, lend an essentially Creole flavour to this American variation of bouillabaisse from the southern state of Louisiana. Crisp garlic croûtes are the perfect accompaniment.

1 Make croûtes (see box, page 89), rubbing the top side of the croûtes with 1–2 peeled garlic cloves before toasting.
2 Prepare and marinate the white fish and oily fish as directed in the main recipe. Peel 500 g (1 lb) scampi or large prawns. Slice the green parts of 3 spring onions.
3 Make the bouillabaisse broth as directed in the main recipe, omitting the sprigs of parsley and adding 5 ml (1 tsp) cayenne pepper and 5 ml (1 tsp) dried thyme with the orange zest.
4 Cook the fish in the broth as directed, adding the scampi, the spring onions, and a dozen shelled oysters with their liquid at the same time as the white fish pieces.
5 Serve the fish and broth in individual soup plates, with the garlic croûtes. Garnish with oysters in their shells, if you like.

Spicy mayonnaise can be added to each portion to taste

GETTING AHEAD

The bouillabaisse broth can be made up to 8 hours ahead and kept in the refrigerator. The fish should be cooked in the broth just before serving.

SAUTEED TROUT WITH HAZELNUTS

🍽 SERVES 4　🥣 WORK TIME 20–25 MINUTES　🍲 COOKING TIME 10–15 MINUTES

EQUIPMENT

palette knife

small knife

kitchen scissors

chef's knife　oval fish pan†

wooden spoon

paper towels

aluminium foil

baking sheet

chopping board

† large frying pan can also be used

In this quick recipe, trout are lightly dusted with seasoned flour, then pan-fried in butter and topped with a mixture of sautéed, toasted hazelnuts and chopped parsley. The crunchy topping makes a delicious contrast with the soft textured flesh of the trout, and thin slices of lemon add a fresh accent to the dish. The subtle nutty flavour of a rice pilaf, such as the one on page 74, would marry well with the hazelnuts.

GETTING AHEAD

The trout and hazelnuts are best prepared and sautéed just before serving.

metric	SHOPPING LIST	imperial
4	trout, weighing about 300 g (10 oz) each, cleaned and scaled	4
60 g	hazelnuts	2 oz
5–7	sprigs of parsley	5–7
2	lemons	2
20–30 g	plain flour	³/₄–1 oz
	salt and pepper	
125 g	butter	4 oz

INGREDIENTS

trout †

hazelnuts　　　butter

parsley

plain flour

lemons

† other suitable fish
mackerel, red mullet

ANNE SAYS
"Ask your fishmonger to clean the trout through the gills rather than the stomach, to keep their shape better. Or you can do this yourself – see the box on page 113."

ORDER OF WORK

1 PREPARE THE TROUT

2 PREPARE THE GARNISH

3 COOK THE TROUT; FINISH THE DISH

1 PREPARE THE TROUT

Trimming makes
fish more attractive
to serve whole

1 Cut the fins from the trout with the
scissors, and trim the tails to a "V".
Rinse the fish inside and out, and pat
dry with paper towels.

Snip off fins
with scissors

2 PREPARE THE GARNISH

Skins rub off
easily from
warm hazelnuts

Hazelnuts will add
texture to trout

1 Heat the oven
to 180°C (350°F,
Gas 4). Spread the
hazelnuts on the baking
sheet and toast them until
browned, 8–10 minutes. While
still hot, rub the hazelnuts in a tea
towel to remove the skins. Let cool.

2 Using the chef's knife, chop the
toasted hazelnuts coarsely.

3 Strip the parsley leaves from
the stalks and pile them on the
chopping board. With the chef's knife,
chop the leaves coarsely.

4 Trim the ends from 1 of the
lemons, then halve the lemon
lengthwise and cut it into thin
semi-circles, leaving the skin intact.

5 Peel the second lemon (see box,
page 98, step 1). Turn the lemon
on its side and cut it into thin rounds.
Remove any pips.

HOW TO PEEL AND SEGMENT A LEMON

Segment lemons using this method to leave only crescents of flesh.

1 Trim the ends from the lemon. Set the fruit upright and cut away the skin and white pith, following the curve of the fruit.

2 With the lemon in your hand, slide a knife down one side of a segment, cutting it from the skin. Cut down the other side; pull out the segment. Repeat with the remaining segments. Discard pips.

ANNE SAYS
"*Segment the lemon over a bowl to catch the juice.*"

COOK THE TROUT; FINISH THE DISH

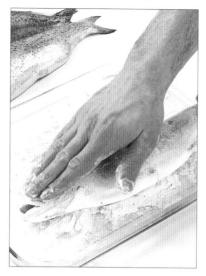

1 Put the flour on a large plate and season with salt and pepper. Coat each trout with the seasoned flour, patting with your hands so each fish is evenly coated.

3 Using the palette knife, turn the trout over and continue cooking over low heat.

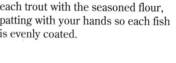

Turn fish carefully to avoid breaking crisp skin

2 Heat half of the butter in the fish pan until it is foaming. Add 2 of the prepared fish to the pan and brown them over medium heat, 2–3 minutes.

4 When ready, the trout will be browned and the flesh will flake easily when tested with a fork, 3–5 minutes. Transfer the fish to a warmed platter and cover with foil to keep warm.

ANNE SAYS
"*When testing if the fish are done, first make a small cut near the head where the flesh is thickest.*"

5 Cook the remaining 2 trout, using the rest of the butter. Add the fish to the 2 on the platter, and cover them again with foil.

6 Add the hazelnuts to the fish pan and sauté over medium heat until they are golden brown, stirring constantly, 3–4 minutes.

7 Add three-quarters of the parsley to the pan and stir to mix it with the nuts and browned butter.

Butter should be golden brown so it increases nutty flavour

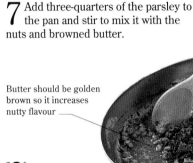

🍴 TO SERVE
Transfer the fish to warmed individual plates, and spoon the hazelnut and parsley mixture over the trout. Decorate with the lemon semi-circles and rounds. Sprinkle with the remaining chopped parsley.

Parsley and hazelnut **garnish** enhances flavour of freshly caught trout

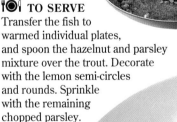

Rice pilaf is a good contrast to butter sauce on trout

VARIATION

SAUTEED TROUT WITH CAPERS, LEMON, AND CROUTONS

Small croûtons provide the crunch in this piquant garnish for sautéed trout.

1 Peel and segment 3 lemons (see box, page 98). Cut the lemon segments into 3–4 pieces each and gently mix with 30 ml (2 tbsp) drained capers.
2 Trim the crusts from 2 slices of white bread. Cut the bread into small cubes about the size of the capers.
3 Prepare and cook the trout as directed in the main recipe, using 60 g (2 oz) butter. Transfer them to a platter, cover, and keep warm.
4 Wipe out the pan. Add another 75 g (2½ oz) butter and fry the bread cubes until golden, 1–2 minutes.
5 Add the capers and pieces of lemon, season with salt and pepper, and swirl to combine.
6 Pour the mixture over the fish. Decorate with lemon semi-circles and parsley sprigs and serve at once.

POACHED SALMON WITH WATERCRESS SAUCE

🍽 SERVES 4–6   🥄 WORK TIME 25–30 MINUTES   🍲 POACHING TIME 15–20 MINUTES

EQUIPMENT

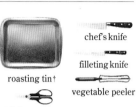
roasting tin†

chef's knife

filleting knife

vegetable peeler

kitchen scissors

small knife

tweezers

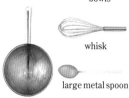
bowls

whisk

large metal spoon

colander

lemon squeezer

paper towels

aluminium foil

chopping board

† fish poacher or long deep
flameproof dish can also be used

*Poaching in a court bouillon, an aromatic liquid,
is an ideal way to cook a whole salmon or salmon
trout, adding flavour and keeping it moist.
Ask your fishmonger to clean the fish through
the stomach.*

INGREDIENTS

fresh
salmon†

carrot

lemon

watercress

onion

plain
yogurt

bouquet
garni

Tabasco
sauce

dry white
wine

double
cream

peppercorns

† other suitable fish
bass, salmon trout

metric	SHOPPING LIST	imperial
1.8 kg	fresh salmon, cleaned through the stomach	4 lb
	salt and pepper	
	For the court bouillon	
1	onion	1
1	carrot	1
6	peppercorns	6
250 ml	dry white wine	8 fl oz
1.5 litres	water, more if needed	2½ pints
1	bouquet garni made with 5–6 parsley stalks, 2–3 sprigs of fresh thyme, and 1 bay leaf	1
	For the watercress sauce	
1	bunch of watercress	1
250 ml	double cream	8 fl oz
250 ml	plain yogurt	8 fl oz
1	lemon	1
	Tabasco sauce	

ORDER OF WORK

1 MAKE THE COURT BOUILLON

2 PREPARE AND POACH THE SALMON

3 MAKE THE SAUCE

4 FINISH THE SALMON

1 MAKE THE COURT BOUILLON

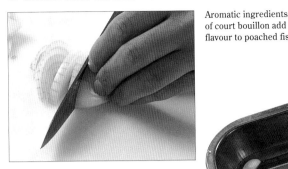

Aromatic ingredients of court bouillon add flavour to poached fish

1 Peel the onion, leaving a little of the root attached, and cut it in half through root and stalk. Lay each onion half flat on the chopping board and cut across into medium slices.

2 Peel the carrot and cut it across into medium slices.

3 Combine the onion, carrot, peppercorns, white wine, water, and 5 ml (1 tsp) salt in the roasting tin. Add the bouquet garni. Bring to a boil and simmer 20 minutes. Let cool. Meanwhile, prepare the salmon (see page 102).

HOW TO TRIM A FISH

When serving fish whole, trim the fins with kitchen scissors so they do not interfere with serving, and cut the tail into a "V" shape.

1 Cut the fins from both sides of the fish, then from its belly.

2 Turn the fish over and cut the fins from along the back of the fish.

3 Cut a triangle from the tail of the fish to make a neat "V" in the tail.

PREPARE AND POACH THE SALMON

1 Scale the salmon (see box, below), then trim the fish (see box, page 101). Using the filleting knife, slit between the ribcage bones and flesh.

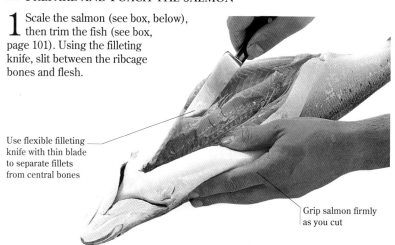

Use flexible filleting knife with thin blade to separate fillets from central bones

Grip salmon firmly as you cut

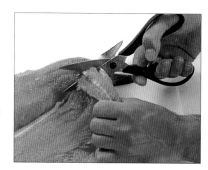

2 Work towards the backbone, loosening the flesh from the bones on both sides of the ribcage without cutting the skin.

3 Using the scissors, snip the bone at the head to release it. Pull the bone out from the head end.

4 Snip the bone at the tail end to release it. Cut the bone into pieces and reserve. With the tweezers, remove any visible bones from the fish, then run your fingers along the inside of the fish to check that all have been removed.

Rinse raw fish before cooking to wash away any remaining impurities

HOW TO SCALE A FISH

Most fish must be scaled before cooking, though often you will find that your fishmonger has done this. Some fish, such as freshwater trout, have small scales that do not need to be removed. A few fish, such as shark, do not have scales at all.

Fish scales will scatter, so work over draining board or even outdoors

Using the back of a filleting knife, a fish scaler, or a serrated knife held at an angle, scrape off the scales from the whole fish, working from tail to head. Rinse the fish under running water and dry well with paper towels.

5 Rinse the fish inside and out with cold water and pat dry with paper towels.

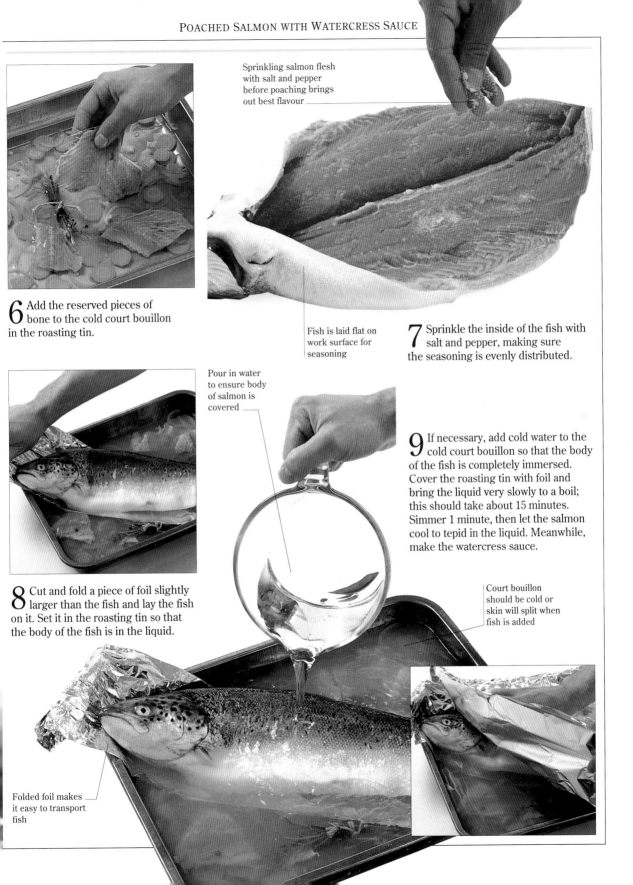

Sprinkling salmon flesh with salt and pepper before poaching brings out best flavour

6 Add the reserved pieces of bone to the cold court bouillon in the roasting tin.

Fish is laid flat on work surface for seasoning

7 Sprinkle the inside of the fish with salt and pepper, making sure the seasoning is evenly distributed.

Pour in water to ensure body of salmon is covered

9 If necessary, add cold water to the cold court bouillon so that the body of the fish is completely immersed. Cover the roasting tin with foil and bring the liquid very slowly to a boil; this should take about 15 minutes. Simmer 1 minute, then let the salmon cool to tepid in the liquid. Meanwhile, make the watercress sauce.

8 Cut and fold a piece of foil slightly larger than the fish and lay the fish on it. Set it in the roasting tin so that the body of the fish is in the liquid.

Court bouillon should be cold or skin will split when fish is added

Folded foil makes it easy to transport fish

3 MAKE THE SAUCE

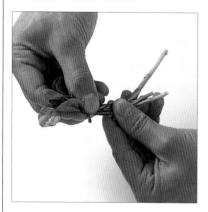

1 Divide the sprigs of the watercress, then wash them in the colander and dry them thoroughly. Strip the leaves from the stalks.

2 Pile the watercress leaves on the chopping board and chop them, using the chef's knife.

3 Whip the cream until soft peaks form. In another bowl, whisk the yogurt until smooth.

Lemon juice gives freshness and tang to watercress sauce

Watercress is coarsely chopped to give texture to sauce

Whipped cream and yogurt form smooth base for sauce

4 Add the yogurt to the whipped cream and stir gently to mix them together thoroughly.

5 Add the chopped watercress and a dash of Tabasco sauce. Cut the lemon in half. Squeeze the juice from each half and add to the sauce.

6 Stir the sauce until evenly blended. Add salt and pepper to taste. Cover the bowl and chill until ready to serve.

FINISH THE SALMON

1 Holding the ends of the foil, carefully lift the salmon out of the liquid; let drain. Lift the fish off the foil.

Grasp ends of foil firmly to remove salmon from cooking liquid

2 Using the small knife, slit the skin neatly around the head. Repeat around the tail.

3 Peel off the skin from the body, pulling it gently with the help of the small knife. Leave the head and tail intact. Scrape along the back ridge of the fish to remove the line of bones.

4 Using the small knife, gently scrape off any dark flesh from the length of the salmon.

¶©¶ TO SERVE

Carefully transfer the fish to a large, oval platter and decorate with fresh dill sprigs, salad leaves, tomato wedges, and vegetables, if you like. Serve the watercress sauce separately. Slice the salmon, discarding the head and tail.

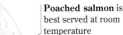

Poached salmon is best served at room temperature

—— GETTING AHEAD ——

The salmon can be poached up to 24 hours ahead and kept, tightly covered, in the refrigerator. Remove the salmon from the refrigerator 20 minutes before serving to allow it to reach room temperature. Peel off the skin just before serving. The watercress sauce can be made up to 4 hours ahead.

Watercress sauce is cool and fresh-tasting

PAN-FRIED MACKEREL COATED IN ROLLED OATS

🍽 SERVES 6   ⌣ WORK TIME 15–20 MINUTES   ☕ FRYING TIME 8–12 MINUTES

EQUIPMENT

saucepans

tweezers

large frying pan   sieve

whisk

tongs   paper towels

greaseproof paper

filleting knife

baking sheet

chopping board

The traditional Scottish recipe for herring, coated with oats and fried, is here adapted using mackerel fillets. For authenticity, use lard or bacon dripping instead of oil for frying. The accompanying mustard sauce is a piquant contrast.

GETTING AHEAD

The fish can be coated up to 2 hours ahead and kept refrigerated. Fry just before serving. The mustard sauce can be made up to 1 hour ahead and kept warm in a bain-marie.

metric	SHOPPING LIST	imperial
3	cleaned mackerel, weighing about 375–500 g (³/₄–1 lb each)	3
75 ml	vegetable oil, more if needed	2¹/₂ fl oz
	salt and pepper	
	slices of lemon and parsley sprigs for decoration	
	For coating the fish	
2	eggs	2
30 g	plain flour	1 oz
175 g	rolled oats	6 oz
	For the mustard sauce	
60 g	butter	2 oz
30 ml	plain flour	2 tbsp
300 ml	boiling water	¹/₂ pint
	juice of ¹/₂ lemon	
15 ml	Dijon mustard, more to taste	1 tbsp

INGREDIENTS

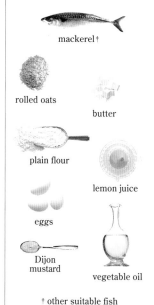

mackerel †

rolled oats

butter

plain flour

lemon juice

eggs

Dijon mustard

vegetable oil

† other suitable fish
whole cleaned and scaled herring

ANNE SAYS
"If you prefer to buy your fish already prepared, you can use 6 skinned mackerel fillets."

ORDER OF WORK

1   **PREPARE AND COAT THE MACKEREL**

2   **MAKE THE MUSTARD SAUCE**

3   **FRY THE MACKEREL**

PAN-FRIED MACKEREL COATED IN ROLLED OATS

HOW TO FILLET A ROUND FISH

Round fish, such as salmon, cod, and mackerel, have 2 fillets that can be cut from either side of the backbone. A well-sharpened filleting knife works best for cutting smooth, even fillets.

1 Starting just behind the head, cut across the fish down to the backbone using a filleting knife.

Hold fish securely with other hand

2 Set the fish on the work surface so that the tail is towards you. Slit the skin along the back from head to tail, holding the knife horizontally.

3 Slide the knife along the upper side of the backbone, carefully detaching the flesh to the mid-point of the fillet.

ANNE SAYS
"A constant cutting motion helps the fillet remain intact."

4 Continue cutting over the rib cage of the fish to free the flesh from the bones and remove the fillet completely.

5 To remove the second fillet, run the knife under the backbone, from head to tail. Sever the fillet from the bone at the tail. Lift off the bone and sever the fillet at the head.

Slide knife as close as possible to backbone to remove flesh neatly

6 Rinse the fillets in cold water and dry on paper towels. If the fish bones are to be used to make stock, rinse them well and reserve them.

HOW TO REMOVE SKIN FROM A FISH FILLET

In many recipes, dark or tough skin is removed from fish fillets before they are cooked.

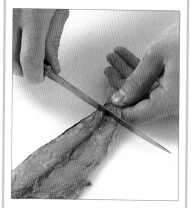

1 Lay the fillet skin-side down on the work surface with the tail end towards you. Holding the tail end firmly with your fingertips, make a small cut through the flesh just to the skin.

2 Angle the knife so that the cutting edge is against the skin and the blade almost parallel to it. Cut the fish flesh away from the skin, working away from you and using a slight sawing motion, still holding the skin firmly with your other hand.

1 PREPARE AND COAT THE MACKEREL

1 Fillet the mackerel (see box, page 107), then skin the fillets (see box, left). Remove any remaining small bones with the tweezers.

Only tender fish flesh remains after fillets have been skinned

Tweezers are precision tool for taking out small bones

2 Rinse the mackerel fillets again with cold water, put on paper towels, and pat dry.

ANNE SAYS
"Once they have been skinned, the mackerel fillets are quite fragile, so handle them gently."

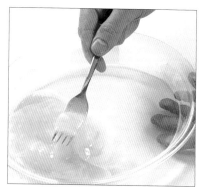

3 Put the eggs into a shallow dish and beat them with 2.5 ml (½ tsp) salt just until mixed. Sift the flour onto a sheet of greaseproof paper.

4 With your fingers, combine the rolled oats, salt, and pepper on a second sheet of greaseproof paper.

5 Turn each of the mackerel fillets in the flour, so that they are evenly coated, then put them on a plate.

Lift edges of paper to roll and toss fish in oats

6 Dip 1 fillet in the beaten egg to coat it, using 2 forks. Transfer to the oat mixture and coat, tossing with the paper to cover. Dip and coat each remaining fillet.

Oat coating sticks to beaten egg

MAKE THE MUSTARD SAUCE

1 Over low heat, slowly melt one-third of the butter in a medium saucepan.

2 Add the flour to the melted butter in the saucepan and whisk to form a smooth paste. Cook until foaming, about 1 minute.

3 Take from the heat and whisk in the boiling water. The sauce will thicken at once.

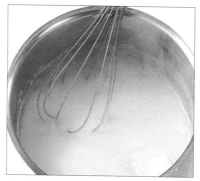

Whisk constantly to prevent lumps forming

4 Return the saucepan to the heat and cook the sauce, whisking constantly, 1 minute. Remove the saucepan from the heat again; add the remaining butter to the sauce and whisk together thoroughly.

5 Add the lemon juice and mustard; whisk to mix. Season to taste with salt, pepper, and more mustard, then whisk again until completely smooth. To keep the sauce warm, set the saucepan in a larger pan of hot water.

! TAKE CARE !

Do not boil or overcook a sauce containing Dijon mustard or it will be bitter.

３ FRY THE MACKEREL

1 Heat the oven to very low to keep the fish warm. Line the baking sheet with paper towels. Heat the oil in the frying pan. Add 3 fillets; cook until crisp and golden on the underside, 2–3 minutes.

Fish is cooked in batches so coating does not get soggy

2 Turn the mackerel fillets with the tongs, being careful not to loosen the oat coating.

Flesh should flake
easily with fork

3 Cook until
golden and the fish
flakes easily when tested with
a fork, 2–3 minutes longer. Transfer
to the lined baking sheet; keep warm in
the oven while you fry the remaining
fillets, adding more oil if necessary.

TO SERVE
Arrange the mackerel fillets on a warmed
platter and decorate with halved, twisted
lemon slices and parsley sprigs.
Serve with the warm mustard
sauce on the side.

Mustard sauce is
perfect partner for
crisp-fried fish

Oat coating is
crunchy contrast to
tender mackerel

VARIATION

ALMOND-COATED RAINBOW TROUT

*Rainbow trout has a sweet-
flavoured flesh that marries
perfectly with almonds.*

1 Omit the mustard sauce
from the main recipe.
  2 Chop 175 g (6 oz) flaked
  almonds and season with salt
and pepper.
  3 Rinse and pat dry 6 skinned
  trout fillets (175 g/6 oz each).
  Coat as for the mackerel in
  the main recipe, substituting
  the chopped almonds for the
  rolled oats.
  4 Pan-fry the fish as directed,
  over low heat so the almond
  coating does not burn, allowing
3–4 minutes on each side.
5 Cut the trout fillets into pieces
and arrange in a decorative pattern on
warmed individual plates.
6 Serve the fillets with potatoes
sautéed in butter and scattered with
a few chopped chives, if you like.

GRILLED TROUT WITH ORANGE AND MUSTARD GLAZE

🍽 SERVES 6   🥄 WORK TIME 15–20 MINUTES   🍲 GRILLING TIME 20–30 MINUTES

EQUIPMENT

chef's knife

filleting knife   small knife

kitchen scissors

palette knife

paper towels

tongs

pastry brush

whisk

small bowl

chopping board

ANNE SAYS
"Kitchen scissors for preparing fish should have straight blades and must be strong enough to cut through fish skin and fins."

Grilled whole fish is a dream, quick to prepare and easy to present. Small fish are best because their bones keep them moist and their skin protects them from the intense heat. You can also barbecue the fish, but choose the fuel carefully; strongly flavoured wood such as pine can overpower white-fleshed fish.

GETTING AHEAD

The glaze can be made up to 1 week ahead and kept refrigerated. The fish and vegetables can be prepared up to 2 hours ahead, but grill them just before serving.

INGREDIENTS

trout †

honey   Dijon mustard

fresh tarragon

vegetable oil

orange juice   tomatoes

mushrooms   onions

†other suitable fish
bream

ORDER OF WORK

1 PREPARE THE FISH

2 PREPARE THE VEGETABLES; MAKE THE GLAZE

3 GRILL THE VEGETABLES AND FISH

metric	SHOPPING LIST	imperial
6	trout, each weighing 375 g (12 oz)	6
6–8	sprigs of fresh tarragon	6–8
3	large sweet onions	3
3	ripe medium tomatoes	3
250 g	mushrooms	8 oz
45–60 ml	vegetable oil for grill rack	3–4 tbsp
	For the orange and mustard glaze	
60 ml	Dijon mustard	4 tbsp
10 ml	honey	2 tsp
135 ml	orange juice, from 2 oranges	4¹/₂ fl oz
60 ml	vegetable oil	4 tbsp
	salt and pepper	

...the Biggest Name in American Water *Culligan.*

Eliminate:
- Staining
- Turbidity
- Nitrates
- Bacteria

- Acid Water
- Rotten Egg Odor
- Bad Taste
- Chlorine

- Hard Water
- Radium
- Cloudy Ice Cubes
- Spotty Dishes

** The substances removed by these systems are not necessarily in your water.

With:
- Conditioners
- Softeners

- Reverse Osmosis
- Acid Neutralizers

- Carbon Filters
- Filtration

Call For A **FREE** Water Analysis Today!!
1-877-427-8985

Rent/Purchase any *Culligan.* system and take $100 off the Installation

AND

Dinner for 2 at Outback Steakhouse on *Culligan.* (Purchase/rent any system and receive a $50 gift certificate to Outback Steakhouse)

** Coupons must be presented at the time of FREE water analysis or system purchase. May not be used in conjunction with any other offer. Since *Culligan.* dealers are independently operated, offer and participation may vary.

Culligan

THE WATER EXPERTS ®

OFFER EXPIRES ON OCTOBER 3, 2003

Healthy,

Clear,

Clean...

0280 ****************ECRWSS**R013
RESIDENT
RURAL ROUTE R013
EDGEWATER MD 21037

1 PREPARE THE FISH

2 Strip the tarragon leaves from the stalks, then tuck a leaf of tarragon in each slash. Set the fish aside in a cool place.

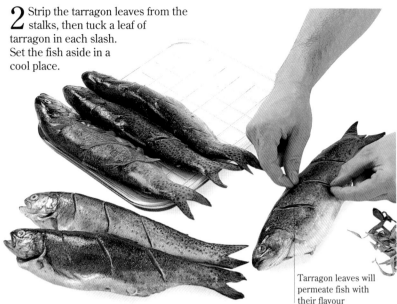

1 Clean the fish through the gills (see box, below). With the scissors, cut the fins from the fish and trim the tails to a "V". Rinse the fish inside and out and pat dry with paper towels. With the filleting knife, slash each fish diagonally 3–4 times on both sides. Make the slashes about 1 cm (¹/₂ inch) deep to allow heat to penetrate.

Tarragon leaves will permeate fish with their flavour

HOW TO CLEAN A WHOLE FISH THROUGH THE GILLS

Fish to be served whole are cleaned through the gills in order to maintain their shape. If the fish is cleaned by your fishmonger, make sure you specify "through the gills". If the stomach is cut open, it will curl unattractively during cooking.

Cold running water cleans stomach cavity thoroughly

1 Hook your fingers through the gills and pull them out.

2 Reach through the gill opening and pull out the stomach contents.

! TAKE CARE !
The gills can be quite sharp so be careful when putting in your fingers.

3 With scissors, make a small slit at the ventral or stomach opening and pull out any remaining contents.

4 Run cold water into the gill opening and out through the ventral opening to clean the cavity thoroughly.

2 PREPARE THE VEGETABLES; MAKE THE GLAZE

1 Peel the onions and cut them crosswise into 1 cm (½ inch) slices, discarding the root and top.

2 Cut the cores from the tomatoes, then cut each one crosswise in half. Wipe the mushroom caps with a damp paper towel and trim the stalks even with the caps.

3 Make the glaze: whisk the Dijon mustard and honey together in the bowl, then whisk in the orange juice. Gradually pour in the oil, whisking constantly. Season with salt and pepper.

3 GRILL THE VEGETABLES AND FISH

1 Heat the grill. Brush the rack generously with oil. Arrange the onion slices and mushrooms on the rack. Brush them with a little of the glaze and sprinkle with salt and pepper.

Brush glaze to edge of each onion slice

Honey-mustard glaze moistens vegetables and grills to golden finish

2 Grill the onions and mushrooms about 7.5 cm (3 inches) from the heat, brushing with a little more glaze and turning occasionally with the tongs, allowing about 3 minutes for the mushrooms and 5–7 minutes for the onions; they should be slightly charred. Remove and keep warm.

3 Cook the tomatoes skin-side towards the heat until warmed through and the skin is slightly charred, 5–7 minutes; do not turn them. Remove and keep warm.

4 Place the fish on the rack (in 2 batches if necessary). Brush with glaze; sprinkle with salt and pepper. Grill until browned, 4–7 minutes.

Flake flesh gently with fork to test

5 Carefully turn the fish using the palette knife, and brush each with more glaze. Continue grilling until the flesh just flakes easily when tested with a fork, 4–7 minutes more.

ANNE SAYS

"Cooking time depends on the thickness of the fish, measured at the thickest point. For every 2.5 cm (1 inch) of thickness, allow 10 minutes cooking time."

Crispy trout skin is coated with delicious honey-mustard glaze

🍽 **TO SERVE**

Place the fish on warmed individual plates and serve with the vegetables, and a decoration of lamb's lettuce, if you like. Spoon any remaining glaze over the fish.

VARIATION

GRILLED COD STEAKS WITH MAITRE D'HOTEL BUTTER

These grilled cod steaks are topped with pats of butter flavoured with parsley, shallot, and lemon.

1 Omit the glaze. Peel 1 shallot and set it flat-side down on a chopping board. Slice horizontally towards the root, leaving the slices attached at the root. Slice vertically, then cut across the shallot to make fine dice.

2 Strip the leaves from 8–10 parsley stalks and pile them on the chopping board. Finely chop the leaves.

3 Cream 75 g (2½ oz) butter. Mix in the chopped shallot and parsley, the juice of ½ lemon, salt, and pepper. Spoon the butter onto a piece of greaseproof paper and shape it into a roll, twisting the ends to seal. Refrigerate until firm.

4 Rinse and dry 6 cod steaks (total weight 1.2 kg/2½ lb). Brush with 45–60 ml (3–4 tbsp) olive oil, sprinkle with salt and pepper, and grill 3–5 minutes on each side. After turning, brush with more olive oil and sprinkle with more salt and pepper.

5 Set a slice of the maître d'hôtel butter on top of each cod steak and serve, accompanied by grated carrot with a scattering of dill, if you like.

SOLE BONNE FEMME

EQUIPMENT

bowls

chef's knife

filleting knife

frying pan

pastry brush

kitchen scissors

baking dish

saucepans

wooden spoon

fish slice

whisk

large metal spoon

ladle

chopping board

aluminium foil

sieve

paper towels

In this most delicious of fish dishes, fillets of sole are poached in fish stock, which forms the basis for a creamy velouté sauce. The bones from the filleted sole can be used for the fish stock.

GETTING AHEAD
The fish can be filleted and the fish stock prepared up to 4 hours in advance. Keep in the refrigerator until needed, making sure the fish is covered.

metric	SHOPPING LIST	imperial
2	Dover sole, 1 kg (2 lb) each, cleaned and scaled	2
2	shallots	2
250 g	mushrooms	8 oz
15 g	butter, more for baking dish and foil	½ oz
	salt and pepper	
45–60 ml	water	3–4 tbsp
	For the fish stock	
1	onion	1
500 ml	cold water, more if needed	16 fl oz
3–5	sprigs of parsley	3–5
5 ml	peppercorns	1 tsp
250 ml	white wine or juice of 1 lemon	8 fl oz
	For the sauce	
30 g	butter	1 oz
30 ml	plain flour	2 tbsp
45 ml	double cream	3 tbsp
3	egg yolks	3
	juice of ½ lemon, or to taste	

INGREDIENTS

Dover sole †

egg yolks

double cream

white wine

butter

mushrooms

plain flour

shallots

parsley

peppercorns

onion

lemon juice

† other suitable fish
halibut, lemon sole

ORDER OF WORK

1 PREPARE THE SOLE

2 MAKE THE FISH STOCK

3 PREPARE THE MUSHROOMS; POACH THE SOLE

4 MAKE THE SAUCE AND FINISH THE DISH

1 PREPARE THE SOLE

Lay fish flat on
work surface for
filleting

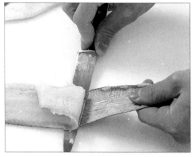

Cut neatly to outline
fillet shape

1 Fillet the sole (see box,
page 118), reserving the
washed heads and bones to make
the fish stock.

2 Set each fillet skin-side down and
hold the tail firmly. Cut through
to the skin at the tail end, then angle
the knife, and cut the flesh from the
skin, using a sawing motion. Rinse the
fillets and pat dry with paper towels.

2 MAKE THE FISH STOCK

Stock is clear
and light if
bones are
washed well

1 Cut the washed fish heads and
bones into 4–5 pieces with the
chef's knife.

2 Peel the onion, leaving a little of
the root attached, and cut it in half
through root and stalk. Cut each half
vertically into thin slices.

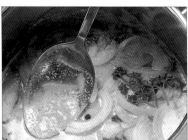

3 Put the fish heads and bones in a
medium saucepan. Add the onion,
water, parsley, and peppercorns. Pour
in the wine.

4 Bring to a boil and simmer
about 20 minutes, skimming
occasionally with the large spoon.

! TAKE CARE !
*Do not simmer the stock too long or
it will be bitter.*

5 Pour the fish stock through the
sieve into a second saucepan,
to remove all flavouring ingredients.

ANNE SAYS
*"Do not season the stock as the flavours
will intensify when it is reduced."*

HOW TO FILLET A FLATFISH

Flatfish, such as sole and flounder, are usually cut into four fillets, two on either side of the central bones. The filleting technique is quite similar to that used for round fish.

1 With the point of a filleting knife, cut around the edge of the fish to outline the shape of the fillets. With the point of the knife, cut the fish to the bone in a semicircle behind the head.

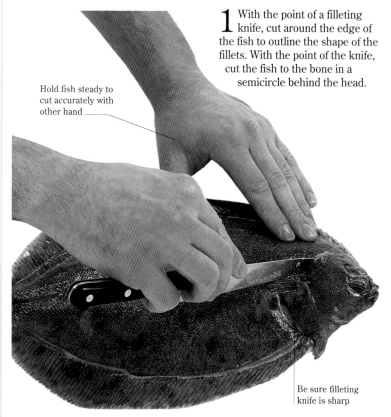

Hold fish steady to cut accurately with other hand

Be sure filleting knife is sharp

2 Cut through to the bone, along the spine at the centre of the fish, in a straight line from head to tail.

3 Keeping the knife almost flat, slip the blade between the flesh and the rib bones and cut away the fillet, using a stroking motion.

4 Continue cutting until the fillet and flesh lying along the fins are detached with the skin in one piece. Turn the fish around and slip the knife under the flesh of the second fillet. Detach the fillet from the bones as for the first fillet.

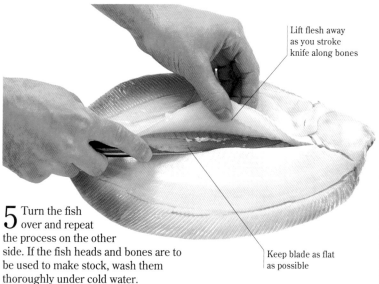

Lift flesh away as you stroke knife along bones

5 Turn the fish over and repeat the process on the other side. If the fish heads and bones are to be used to make stock, wash them thoroughly under cold water.

Keep blade as flat as possible

3 PREPARE THE MUSHROOMS; POACH THE SOLE

1 Heat the oven to 180°C (350°F, Gas 4). Peel the shallots and separate into sections, if necessary. Slice horizontally towards the root, then slice vertically, leaving the root end uncut; cut across to make fine dice.

2 Wipe the mushroom caps with a damp paper towel and trim the stalks even with the caps. Set the mushrooms stalk-side down on the chopping board and slice them.

3 Melt the butter in the frying pan; add the mushrooms with salt, pepper, and water. Cover with buttered foil and cook until the mushrooms are tender when tested with the small knife, 5 minutes. Set aside.

Fillets should not be completely immersed in stock

4 Butter the baking dish; sprinkle the shallots over the bottom. Fold each sole fillet in half, with the skinned side inwards, and arrange on the shallots, tail upwards. Season the fish with salt and pepper.

5 Ladle enough fish stock over the fillets to half cover them. Top with a piece of buttered foil.

6 Poach the fish in the heated oven until it just flakes easily when tested with a fork, 15–18 minutes.

7 Using the fish slice, transfer each sole fillet to paper towels to drain, reserving the fish cooking liquid. Keep the fillets warm while making the sauce.

4 MAKE THE SAUCE AND FINISH THE DISH

1 Add the fish cooking liquid with the shallots to the remaining stock; boil until reduced to 375 ml (12 fl oz).

2 Melt the butter in a separate saucepan. Whisk in the flour. Cook until foaming, 1–2 minutes. Remove the pan from the heat and let cool slightly.

3 Strain the reduced stock into the butter and flour mixture. Return to the heat and bring to a boil, whisking constantly until thickened. Reduce the heat and let simmer 5 minutes.

Mushroom slices add essential flavour and make attractive decoration for final dish

5 Mix the cream and egg yolks in a small bowl, using the whisk.

4 Remove the sauce from the heat. Add the mushrooms with their cooking liquid and stir to mix.

6 Ladle a little of the hot sauce into the cream and egg yolk mixture and whisk to mix.

7 Stir the cream mixture into the remaining sauce in the pan. Return to the heat and cook gently, stirring, until it thickens enough to coat the back of the spoon (your finger will leave a trail across the spoon), 2–3 minutes. Do not boil the sauce or it will curdle. Remove from the heat. Add lemon juice, salt, and pepper to taste.

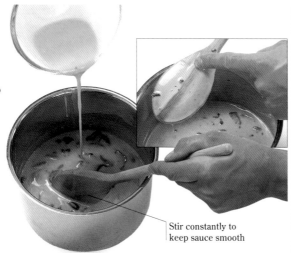

Stir constantly to keep sauce smooth

8 Heat the grill. Arrange 2 fillets on each of 4 flameproof plates. Ladle the sauce over the fish, so it is completely coated. Grill until lightly browned and glazed, 1–2 minutes.

¶◉¶ TO SERVE

Serve the sole at once, garnished with sprigs of fresh herbs, if you like. Boiled rice is an excellent accompaniment.

Boiled rice is perfect with rich sauce and can be shaped neatly in a timbale mould

Creamy velouté sauce complements delicate fish flavour

FILLETS OF SOLE WITH MUSHROOMS AND TOMATOES

Poached sole fillets with a mushroom and tomato-speckled sauce are a colourful variation of Sole Bonne Femme.

1 Cut the cores from 2 tomatoes and score an "x" on the base of each with the tip of a knife. Immerse them in boiling water until the skin starts to split, 8–15 seconds depending on their ripeness. Transfer at once to a bowl of cold water. When cold, peel off the skin. Cut the tomatoes crosswise in half and squeeze out the seeds. Finely chop each half.
2 Prepare the sole, fish stock, and mushrooms as directed.
3 Poach the sole fillets as directed, adding the tomatoes to the baking dish with the shallots.
4 Strip the leaves from 10–12 parsley sprigs and pile them on a chopping board. Finely chop the leaves.
5 Make the sauce, adding the fish cooking liquid to 125 ml (4 fl oz) white wine instead of the remaining stock. Pour the reduced liquid into the butter and flour mixture without straining. When the sauce thickens, whisk in 22.5 ml (1^1/$_2$ tbsp) tomato purée.
6 Add the chopped parsley with the mushrooms and their liquid.
7 Ladle the sauce over the fish arranged on flameproof plates and grill as directed. Serve with custard squashes, if you like.

FISH KNOW-HOW

The wide variety of fish on the market allows the cook an abundant choice. However, different types of fish have different characteristics, and it is helpful to be aware of appropriate substitutes. Because fish is a highly perishable food it is also important to know the best methods for storage and handling. Fish lends itself to many cooking methods and its delicate texture means that microwaving can be an ideal treatment.

CHOOSING FISH

The first rule when buying is to select fish that looks fresh. Luckily, a fish in impeccable condition is easy to spot. Look for the following features:

• Fish should smell fresh and clean, without a strong or unpleasant "fishy" odour.

• For whole fish, the scales should be intact and shiny, the eyes clear and full with no cloudiness, and the gills should be bright pink or red, not dull or brown.

• All fish should feel firm and resilient, not soft or spongy, when pressed with a fingertip.

• Fish fillets should not be dry or discoloured, nor should they be wet or watery. The flesh should have a bright, translucent clarity.

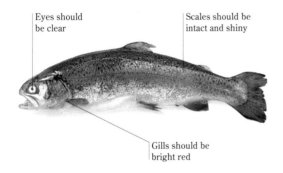

Eyes should be clear

Scales should be intact and shiny

Gills should be bright red

ANNE SAYS
"*A fish that has been cut into steaks or fillets deteriorates more rapidly than a whole fish because the exposed flesh is more vulnerable to bacteria. For this reason it is better to buy fish from a fishmonger who prepares portions on the spot rather than buying pre-cut fish steaks and fillets. Better still, purchase whole fish and cut fillets yourself, because whole fish will remain fresher longer.*"

FISH GROUPS

Fish is almost the only remaining food that is caught mainly in the wild rather than being farmed. As a result, supplies are unpredictable, varying enormously in type and quality from season to season and area to area. Therefore when you shop for fish, you may not always find the fish you want. It is important to know which fish can be substituted for others, and suggestions for alternative fish are given in each recipe. Salmon and trout are farmed, so you are more likely to find them on a consistent basis.

Most important for cooking fish is an understanding of the differences in taste, texture, and bone structure among the various types. A fish with oily, rich flesh is as different from a white-fleshed fish as duck is from chicken. Texture is another important characteristic: the coarse flesh of cod differs from the fine texture of sole and neither could be confused with the firmness of tuna or the delicate pink flesh of salmon.

When you substitute one fish for another in a recipe, it is important to keep the following groups in mind so you can choose a fish that is most appropriate in texture and flavour for the given preparation.

COD FAMILY

Cod, haddock, hake, and pollack are all members of the same family and form almost half of the world's commercial fish catch. Usually too large to sell whole, they are most often cut into steaks or fillets. They resemble one another in many respects, with white, firm flesh which produces large flakes. Not only are these fish abundant, but they yield full-flavoured, thick flesh that is highly adaptable. Fish in the cod family are excellent grilled, sautéed, steamed, baked, or deep-fried with any number of sauces and accompaniments. You can substitute one for another without hesitation.

FLATFISH

Most types of small flatfish (plaice, sole, dab, and flounder) look very alike and can be easily substituted one for another. Flatfish, as the name suggests, are flat, with a lateral bone structure and spine that produce four fillets, unlike the two fillets of all round fish. Many flatfish weigh 375–500 g (12 oz–1 lb) and are ideal as an individual serving on the bone; they can be pan-fried whole or simply scored and baked in the oven with parsley, a little butter, and some white wine.

Halibut and turbot are the only large flatfish that are commonly available. They are sold as steaks or fillets. The flesh of all flatfish is delicate and fine-textured, best left to simple preparations such as poaching, baking, and pan-frying.

FIRM WHITE FISH

Many popular fish have flesh that is white in colour and mild in flavour. Red snapper, grouper, and Hawaiian mahi mahi (also called dolphin fish) are among the fish from this varied  group that offer succulent firm flesh with an excellent flavour. The size of these white fish varies enormously, with some species being small enough to cook whole, while others are sold only cut in fillets and steaks because they are so large. Their firm flesh makes them appropriate for all cooking methods.

MEATY FISH

Two well-known fish, tuna and swordfish, highlight this category, and are inter-changeable in many recipes. Tuna is a rich fish that must be eaten as fresh as possible, particularly darker types. Albacore, the only white-fleshed tuna, is preferred for canning. Swordfish, also white-fleshed, is always sold in steaks, while depending on the variety, tuna comes as steaks or in big pieces resembling a cut of meat. Grilling and barbecuing are favourite methods for cooking both of these meaty fish, with roasting and pan-frying as alternatives.

MONKFISH

This fish, also called anglerfish, has a huge unattractive head and gaping mouth, so you will find only the tail meat on sale, either whole, in fillets, or in steaks. The flesh is mild, slightly sweet, and chewy, and does not overcook easily. Another advantage for the cook is its straight spinal cord: the fact that it has no lateral small bones makes it easy to fillet. Baking and sautéing are good uses for monkfish, and its firm flesh is ideal in fish stews. There is no direct substitute although there are possible alternatives in individual recipes.

SALMON AND TROUT

Salmon and trout look alike and are closely related. Salmon has a deep pink flesh and delectable flavour. It is sold whole, weighing from 2.25–6.75 kg (5–15 lb), and in fillets and steaks. The most familiar variety of trout is rainbow, which is often farmed and sold whole as a single portion (weighing 375–500 g/12 oz–1 lb). Salmon trout has the pink flesh of salmon with the firm texture of trout. The rich flesh of all these fish is ideal for baking, poaching, and sautéing, not to mention barbecuing.

OILY FISH

Fish in this group, such as mackerel, herring, and sardines, tend to have a characteristic flavour. Their flesh is soft and flaky and holds its shape well. Most fish weigh under 500 g (1 lb); sardines are small enough to need several per portion. Absolute freshness is a prerequisite for all oily fish because their high oil content oxidizes and turns rancid rapidly. Despite their richness, they are good pan-fried, since this seals in flavour, and they are also good grilled, baked, or cooked over an open fire. Acid flavourings, such as lemon and vinegar, help to balance their richness, as witness the international popularity of pickled herring.

STORING FISH

Store fresh fish for as short a time as possible. To some extent, shelf-life depends on the type and quality of the fish. A reliable fishmonger is important, so you can be sure of the age of the fish before deciding how long it can be stored at home. Temperature is the key to maintaining quality. Spoilage occurs twice as fast at 4°C (40°F), the usual temperature of a home refrigerator, than at 0°C (32°F), which is the ideal storage temperature for fish, so fish should always be stored in the coldest part of the refrigerator.

Freshly caught whole fish keep longer if they have been gutted because this eliminates the enzymes in the stomach that accelerate decay. Fish fillets and pieces should be used within 24 hours. In general, oily fish, such as mackerel, spoil more rapidly than white fish, such as cod and sole. Fish stored in a home refrigerator should be wrapped tightly in polythene and covered in ice. Note that cut fish should not come into direct contact with ice because this will discolour the flesh and draw out its juices. As the ice melts, take care to drain the water to keep the fish from deteriorating.

FREEZING & THAWING FISH

Freezing fish at home must be done very carefully. Home freezers chill food more slowly than commercial machines, allowing the formation of ice crystals, which penetrate the cell walls of the fish, damaging the flavour and texture. If you must freeze fish, make sure the freezer is set at its lowest temperature. Clean whole fish, and wash it thoroughly, handling it as gently as possible, then wrap it in freezer wrap. Steaks and fillets can also be frozen, carefully wrapped. Rich fish, such as salmon, and firm-fleshed white fish, such as cod, freeze better than delicate ones, such as plaice. If carefully frozen, fish can keep up to 3 months in the freezer.

It is best to thaw frozen fish slowly in the refrigerator before cooking, to maintain texture and minimize moisture loss. Allow a few hours per 500 g (1 lb) of fish. Some cooks like to cook small frozen fish fillets without thawing them; cooking times must be increased accordingly.

FISH STOCK

Fish stock is an indispensable ingredient in many sauces, soups, and chowders. Bones, heads, and tails of lean white fish, especially flatfish, such as sole, are recommended for stock. Avoid rich fish, such as mackerel, that can make stock oily. Fish stock keeps well up to 2 days if it is kept covered in the refrigerator, or it can be frozen.

🍽 MAKES ABOUT 1 LITRE (1¾ PINTS)

🥄 WORK TIME 10–15 MINUTES

🍲 COOKING TIME 20 MINUTES

metric	SHOPPING LIST	imperial
750 g	fish bones and heads	1½ lb
1	onion	1
250 ml	white wine or juice of ½ lemon	8 fl oz
1 litre	water	1¾ pints
3–5	sprigs of parsley	3–5
5 ml	peppercorns	1 tsp

1 Thoroughly wash the fish bones and heads. Cut the bones into 4–5 pieces with a chef's knife. Peel the onion, leaving a little of the root attached, and cut it in half through the root and stalk. Lay each onion half on a chopping board and cut it vertically into thin slices.

2 Put the fish bones and heads in a medium saucepan with the onion slices, wine or lemon juice, water, parsley sprigs, and peppercorns. Bring to a boil and simmer 20 minutes. Skim the stock occasionally with a large metal spoon.

! TAKE CARE !
Do not simmer fish stock too long or it will be bitter.

3 Strain the stock into a bowl. Let cool, then cover and keep in the refrigerator.

ANNE SAYS
"I never season stock with salt and ground pepper at the time of making, because it might be reduced later in individual recipes and the flavours will intensify."

SERVING SIZES

Fish range enormously in size, but when you are buying fresh fish, a few simple guidelines will help you decide how much to buy. For large or individual fish, such as salmon or trout, and small flatfish, such as sole, that are to be served whole on the bone with the head intact, allow 375–500 g (12 oz–1 lb) per person. If the fish is to be served on the bone but with the head removed, count on 250–375 g (8–12 oz) per person. Other factors that influence the size of portions are the leanness of the fish, whether the fish is stuffed, cooked with other ingredients or served with a rich sauce, the role the dish plays within the meal, and the size of appetites. For fillets and steaks that have little or no bone, 175–250 g (6–8 oz) per person is the usual portion.

FISH AND YOUR HEALTH

Low in fat and high in protein, fish has always been a star as far as healthy cooking is concerned. Fish lends itself well to low-calorie methods of cooking, including poaching, steaming, grilling, and barbecuing. *Steamed Fish Plaits with Warm Vinaigrette* is a recipe that is low in fat; you can eliminate the added fat altogether by omitting the warm vinaigrette and serving the fish with a simple squeeze of lemon juice. *Grilled Tuna Steaks with Salsa* has a minimum of added fat, as does *Oriental Halibut in a Paper Case,* and both incorporate a healthy fresh vegetable accompaniment. *Poached Salmon with Watercress Sauce* is yet another healthy choice, served with a yogurt sauce.

The richness of other recipes can be reduced by leaving out accompaniments. Omit the sauces from *Roast Monkfish with Garlic and Chilli Sauces* and enjoy the plainly roasted, herb-coated fish; likewise serve *Bouillabaisse* plain, without the chilli sauce. Cook the *Tuna and Bacon Kebabs* without the bacon; the grilled marinated tuna will be delicious on its own, and lighter without the meat. And don't forget, when frying and sautéing, butter can be replaced with olive or vegetable oil, or with polyunsaturated margarine.

MICROWAVE

Cooking fish is one of the great strengths of the microwave. The speed of the microwave ensures that the naturally delicate flesh of fish stays moist, but also cooks evenly. The texture and flavour of fish are also better preserved than with most conventional cooking methods. For example, you will find that *Steamed Fish Plaits with Warm Vinaigrette* can be cooked more quickly in a microwave than in a steamer, with the same if not better results. *Poached Salmon with Watercress Sauce* cooks in a microwave perfectly – the fish can be curled into a circle for cooking if necessary. *Turbans of Sole with Wild Mushroom Mousse* is yet another recipe that is ideal for cooking in the microwave oven, though don't try to reheat the butter sauce in the microwave once the butter has been added, and make sure the turbans are evenly spaced, and not touching, so that each cooks in the same time. Soups and stews, including *Spicy Fish Stew* and *New England Cod and Mussel Chowder*, can be made very successfully in the microwave.

Many other dishes in this book can be adapted to a combination of microwave and conventional cooking. Sauté the monkfish pieces for *Monkfish Américaine* on top of the stove, then make the Américaine sauce in the microwave. Boil the lasagne noodles for *Seafood Lasagne* conventionally, then cook the assembled dish in the microwave; just before serving, it may need cooking briefly under a hot grill to brown the top. *Fisherman's Pie* can be partially prepared in the microwave, including preparing the sauce and making the mashed potato topping, but do not hard-boil the eggs in the microwave because steam will build up in the shells making them burst. The assembled pie is best baked in the conventional oven.

Here are a few tips to remember when microwaving fish:

• Place thicker fish parts towards the edge of the dish and tuck under thin ends.

• Shield delicate or thin parts of fillets and whole fish with small pieces of very smooth aluminium foil.

• Whole fish, particularly large ones, should be slightly undercooked, then left to stand, covered, because they will continue cooking in their own heat.

• Rotate whole fish or fish fillets during microwaving to ensure even cooking.

• Turn over thick pieces of fish halfway through cooking or the juices that collect in the dish will distribute extra heat to only one side of the fish, cooking it unevenly.

• Excess moisture from microwaved fish can be absorbed by lining the dish with paper towels.

• Do not reheat fish in the microwave; fish cooks so quickly that the flesh will dry out too much.

HOW-TO BOXES

There are pictures of all preparation steps for each **Fish Classics** *recipe. Some basic techniques are general to a number of recipes; they are shown in extra detail in these special "how-to" boxes.*

INDEX

ACKNOWLEDGEMENTS

Photographers David Murray
Jules Selmes
Assisted by Ian Boddy

Chef Eric Treuille
Cookery Consultant Linda Collister
Assisted by Joanna Pitchfork

Typesetting Linda Parker
Rowena Feeny
Robert Moore
Deborah Rhodes
Text film by Disc to Print (UK) Limited

Production Consultant Lorraine Baird

*Carroll & Brown Limited
would like to thank ICTC
(0181 568-4179) for supplying the
Cusinox Elysee pans used throughout the
book, Moulinex Swan Holdings
Limited for the deep-fat fryer.*

*Anne Willan would like to thank
her chief editor Kate Krader, associate
editor Stacy Toporoff, and consultant
editor Cynthia Nims for their vital
help with writing this book and
researching and testing the recipes,
aided by Jacqueline Bobrow and
La Varenne's chefs and trainees.*

NOTES

- Metric and imperial measures have been calculated separately. Only use one set of measures as they are not exact equivalents.

- All spoon measurements are level.

- Spoon measurements are calculated using a standard 5 ml teaspoon and 15 ml tablespoon to give an accurate measurement of small amounts.